Under Pressure: Empowering Cyber Security Incident Responders

Under Pressure: Empowering Cyber Security Incident Responders

3

Foreword

In the rapidly evolving landscape of cybersecurity, where the only constant is change, the role of incident responders has become increasingly critical. As our digital world expands, so does the frequency and sophistication of cyber-attacks, putting organisations and individuals at greater risk. It is with great pleasure and admiration that I introduce this insightful book on Cyber Incident Response, penned by a distinguished expert and a dear friend, Nigel Phair

I have had the privilege of knowing Nigel for many years, witnessing his unwavering dedication to understanding and navigating the intricate challenges posed by cybercrime. This book is a testament to his wealth of knowledge and experience in the field with Australian Federal Police battling cybercrime, providing a comprehensive exploration of incident response in the face of the growing wave of cyber incidents.

Incident response, as dissected in these pages, is not merely a technical process but a complex interplay of human psychology, decision-making, and technical expertise. Nigel skilfully delves into the heart of the matter, exploring the factors that influence the psychological well-being and decision-making of incident responders during a cyber security incident. The inherent time pressure, uncertainty, and the looming spectre of business disruptions and reputational damage add layers of complexity to an already challenging task.

What sets this book apart is its holistic approach. Rather than focusing solely on technical aspects, Nigel takes a generalist perspective, considering the broader implications of incident response. The discussion thoughtfully dissects specific threats such as ransomware, data breaches, and denial-of-service attacks, providing a nuanced understanding of each and their unique challenges.

An especially commendable aspect of this work is the incorporation of the perspectives of the unsung heroes in the cybersecurity realm – the incident responders themselves. Through an anonymous survey, Nigel gathers invaluable insights directly from those on the front lines. This firsthand account adds depth and authenticity to the analysis, enriching the reader's understanding of the challenges faced in the real-world scenarios.

As we navigate the ever-changing landscape of cybersecurity, the insights provided in this book are not only timely but crucial. Organisations and individuals alike will benefit from Nigel's expertise, gaining a deeper understanding of the psychological and decision-making processes that shape the outcomes of cyber security incidents.

In conclusion, I extend my heartfelt congratulations to Nigel on this exceptional contribution to the field of cybersecurity. May this book serve as a guiding light for incident responders, cybersecurity professionals, and organisations seeking to fortify their defences in the face of an escalating cyber threat landscape.

Chathura Abeydeera

Cyber | Space | Intelligence | Resilience

Introduction

Incident response is the process of addressing and mitigating the impact of a cyber-attack or security breach within an organisation, involving detecting and identifying an incident, containing its spread, eradicating the threat, and recovering affected systems while preserving evidence for analysis and future prevention. Globally, the number of cyber incidents is growing exponentially putting a range of stresses on those involved in responding.

According to the Australian Bureau of Statistics, more than 22% of businesses experienced a cyber security attack during the 2021-22 financial year, compared to almost one in 10 (8%) in 2019-20.[1] In the 12 months to June 2022, the Australian Cyber Security Centre received over 76,000 cybercrime reports in the same period, an increase of nearly 13% from the previous financial year. During the 2022-23 financial year, there were nearly 94,000 reports of cybercrime submitted to ReportCyber[1], an increase of 23% compared to the previous financial year. On average, that's one report received every 6 minutes. The cost of cybercrime to businesses increased by 14% compared to the previous financial year. Small businesses experienced an average financial loss of $46,000, while cybercrimes cost medium businesses an average of $97,200, and large businesses an average of $71,600.[2]

---

[1] ReportCyber is a website that allows individuals, businesses, and government agencies to report cybercrime, incidents, or vulnerabilities to the ACSC.

The psychological well-being and decision-making of incident responders during a cyber incident is an important, yet relatively under-developed, area of research. As cyber security attacks continue to be a significant threat to organisations globally, responding to a cyber occurrence can cause significant psychological strain on incident responders, who are responsible for assessing and containing the incident, as well as restoring normal business operations.

Factors such as time pressure, uncertainty, and the potential for data loss or reputational damage can influence the psychological well-being and decision-making of incident responders, which in turn can affect the outcome of the incident. The goal of this publication is to investigate the factors that influence the psychological well-being and decision-making of incident responders during a cyber security incident, and how these factors affect the outcome of the incident.

By understanding the psychological and decision-making processes of incident responders during a cyber security incident, organisations can develop better strategies and support systems to mitigate the impact of these attacks.

This book analyses cyber incident response from a generalist perspective, though it splits out ransomware, data breaches and denial of service attacks in the discussion. It also utilises an anonymous survey of cyber incident responders to get their opinions.

Cybercrime

Invariably, incident response occurs after some type of cybercrime. This may be an external or even an internal attack, however it may not always be malicious, for example a data breach resulting from the careless actions of a staff member. It is however, important to understand what cybercrime and its more popular manifestations are if we are going to understand the myriad of incident activities. Cybercrime refers to criminal activities that are committed using the internet or other forms of digital networks. This phenomenon is impacted due to the reach and impact of cyber attacks generally exceeding that of traditional crimes. Perpetrators of cybercrimes do not require physical proximity to their victims and are not impeded by national borders.

Cybercrime encompasses a wide range of malicious activities that target organisations and individuals. Types of cybercrime commonly faced by individuals and organisations include:

1. Phishing: This involves tricking individuals into revealing sensitive information, such as login credentials or financial details, by impersonating a trusted entity. Attackers often use deceptive emails, messages, or websites to deceive users and gain unauthorised access to systems or steal personal information.

2. Ransomware: A type of malware that usually encrypts files on a victim's computer or network, rendering them inaccessible until a ransom is paid. It can cause significant disruption to an organisations operations and often results in financial loss or even a subsequent data breach.

3. Malware: This refers to malicious software designed to infiltrate systems, steal data, or cause harm. It includes viruses, worms, trojans, spyware, and adware. Malware can be distributed through infected email attachments, malicious downloads, or compromised websites.

4. Data Breach: This occurs when unauthorised individuals gain access to sensitive or confidential information. This can result in the exposure of customer data, intellectual property, trade secrets, or financial records. Breached data is often sold on the dark web or used for identity theft, fraud, or other malicious purposes.

5. Social Engineering: Social engineering involves manipulating individuals through psychological tactics to deceive them into divulging confidential information or performing actions that benefit the attacker. This can include impersonating a trusted person, exploiting human vulnerabilities, or utilising psychological manipulation techniques.

6. Insider Threat: This refers to malicious activities carried out by individuals within an organisation who have authorised access to sensitive data or systems. This can include disgruntled employees, contractors, or partners who misuse their privileges to steal information, disrupt operations, or cause damage.

7. Distributed Denial of Service Attack: This involves overwhelming a target system or network with a flood of traffic, rendering it inaccessible to legitimate users. These attacks can disrupt online services,

cause financial loss, or be used as a diversionary tactic to carry out other cybercrimes.

8. Cyber Espionage: This involves unauthorised access to sensitive information for intelligence gathering or competitive advantage. State-sponsored actors or organised hacking groups often engage in cyber espionage to target government agencies, corporations, or research institutions.

9. Insider Trading and Financial Fraud: Where cyber criminals target organisations to gain access to insider information for illegal trading or manipulate financial systems to carry out fraudulent activities. This includes activities like unauthorised access to stock markets, manipulation of financial data, or compromising trading platforms.

10. Supply Chain Attack: This involves compromising third-party vendors or suppliers to gain unauthorised access to target organisations. Attackers exploit vulnerabilities in the supply chain to introduce malware, backdoors, or other malicious components that can be used to breach the organisation's systems.

It is important for organisations, and subsequently incident responders, to be aware of these various types of cybercrime and implement robust security measures, including employee awareness programs, strong authentication mechanisms, regular software updates, network monitoring, and incident response plans to mitigate the risks associated with cyber threats.

As a result of the above, as more and more activities are conducted online, cybercrime has been and continues to be a rapidly growing problem. The impact of cybercrime can be far-reaching and can affect both individuals and organisations. When reacting to a cyber incident, it is contextually important for responders to understand some of the main impacts including:

1. Financial losses for individuals and organisations, which can include the cost of recovering from a cyber-attack, such as hiring a cyber security firm or paying a ransom, as well as the loss of revenue due to disruption to operations or the theft of sensitive information.

2. Damage to an organisation's reputation, leading to a loss of trust and customers. This is especially damaging for businesses that rely on maintaining a positive image, such as banks or retailers.

3. Loss of personal information such as credit card numbers or Social Security numbers. This can lead to identity theft and financial fraud.

4. Disruption to operations for organisations, leading to downtime and a loss of productivity. This can be especially damaging for businesses that rely on constant access to their systems and data, such as hospitals or manufacturing plants.

5. National security threats by enabling cyber espionage, disruption of critical infrastructure and sabotage of military operations.

6. Psychological impact on individuals, causing stress, anxiety, and a loss of privacy.

A Career in Cyber Security

A career in cyber security is rewarding for several reasons. The field of cyber security continues to experience a talent shortage, which means there are ample job opportunities, particularly for skilled people. As long as cyber threats exist – which with the constant uptake of technology by governments, business and individuals is likely to occur – the need for cyber security professionals will persist. This job security is particularly appealing for many and as a result, cyber security professionals often enjoy competitive salaries and benefits.

Cyber security is a dynamic field that evolves rapidly. Professionals need to be continually learning about new threats, technologies, and defence strategies, making it intellectually stimulating. On top of this is the wide range of roles, from ethical hackers (penetration testers) to incident responders, security analysts, consultants, and more. This variety allows individuals to find a niche that aligns with their interests and strengths.

Cyber security professionals play a critical role in making organisations resilient, knowing this work directly contributes to security and privacy is highly rewarding, especially when combined with the global impact their actions can have, with professionals often working on international incidents and collaborate with experts from around the world.

From a technical perspective a career as a penetration tester allows professionals to use their skills to identify vulnerabilities and improve security, and whilst some might commence their career in this discipline, others progress into leadership roles, such as Chief Information Security Officer or more broadly as a security consultant.

The field is at the forefront of technological innovation. Cyber security professionals are often the first to explore and implement cutting-edge security solutions. This can provide personal fulfillment knowing they are making the digital world safer for everyone. They should take pride in their ability to prevent cyber attacks and protect sensitive data.

There is a strong sense of community among cyber security professionals. Networking opportunities abound through conferences, forums, and professional organisations. A career in cyber security offers both financial rewards and the satisfaction of knowing that you are actively defending against one of the most pressing challenges of the digital age.

Looking after the well-being of cyber security employees is crucial. The nature of cyber security work often involves dealing with high-stress situations, constant monitoring, and responding to security incidents. Neglecting employee well-being can lead to burnout, anxiety, and other mental health issues.

Well-rested and emotionally stable employees are more productive and perform better in their roles. When cyber security professionals are stressed or fatigued – like any other employee – they may make mistakes or overlook critical security threats. Failing to address employee well-being can lead to higher turnover rates, which can be costly in terms of recruitment and training.

Since cyber security employees are at the forefront of protecting an organisation from cyber threats, their ability to respond effectively to incidents may be compromised when they are stressed or experiencing burnout. Similarly, unhappy or disgruntled employees may engage in insider threats, intentionally or unintentionally compromising security. Addressing their well-being may reduce this risk.

Employees who are physically and mentally well are more likely to stay updated on the latest threats and technologies, leading to innovation in security measures. Effective cyber security requires close collaboration between technical and non-technical teams. Well-being programs can improve communication and teamwork and organisations have an ethical responsibility to provide a safe and healthy work environment for their employees.

To address these concerns, organisations should invest in employee well-being programs, provide training on stress management, encourage work-life balance, and create a culture that values mental health. Prioritising the well-being of cyber security employees ultimately leads to stronger security practices and a more resilient organisation, and for the individual, a more satisfying career.

While the importance of well-being applies to all employees, there are specific differences and considerations for cyber security professionals. Cyber security professionals often work in a high-stress environment where they deal with constant threats and pressure to protect sensitive data. The intensity and frequency of these stressors can be unique to their roles.

Investment in continuous training and skill development to help staff stay up-to-date with the latest cyber security techniques and tools, along with training programs can also reduce stress related to feeling unprepared for evolving threats.

Ensuring cyber security teams have adequate resources, including tools and personnel, to perform their duties effectively, whilst also addressing workload issues by distributing tasks evenly and hiring additional staff if necessary is also important.

Other strategies include delivering stress management workshops and training sessions to help employees build resilience and coping strategies, and encouraging regular breaks and relaxation techniques during the workday. Combined with fostering a culture of peer support where team members can share experiences and coping strategies, and establishing employee resource groups focused on mental health and well-being.

Due to the broad range of duties, implementation of a rotation programs which allow staff to switch roles or take on different responsibilities periodically along with cross-training helps prevent burnout by reducing the monotony of daily tasks.

Preparation is key, conducting incident response simulation exercises to help staff practice responding to cyber incidents can help reduce stress during real incidents by enhancing preparedness. Maintaining open and transparent communication with staff about organisational goals, expectations, and security policies, and encouraging feedback and provide a platform for employees to voice concerns.

Recognition and reward of cyber security professionals for their contributions to celebrate successes and milestones will boost morale and motivation. Encouraging staff to take regular breaks during the workday to relax and recharge; provision of comfortable break areas; wellness programs that promote physical health, such as fitness classes or gym memberships are all important as healthy bodies can better cope with stress.

Of course, the organisations leadership should set an example by prioritising their own well-being and work-life balance.   By implementing these programs and actions, organisations can create a supportive and resilient cyber security workforce that is better equipped to handle the demands of the field while maintaining mental and emotional well-being.

Ransomware

A key incident response vector for organisations is as a result of ransomware. Ransomware is a type of malicious software that typically encrypts a victim's files and demands payment, usually in the form of cryptocurrency, to restore access. Ransomware attacks may also result in the theft of information, with the ransomware demand arising from a threat to distribute this information in the public realm.

Usually, this information is sensitive and personally identifying, therefore adding to the pressure to pay. One of the first known instance of ransomware occurred in 1989, when the AIDS Trojan was sent to individuals via floppy disk. The Trojan encrypted the victim's files and displayed a message demanding payment in exchange for the decryption key. The Trojan horse payload would encrypt the names of all directories on drive C: and hide directories and encrypt file names upon the first boot after AIDS is installed. Once the boot count reached 90, the user was asked to renew the license and contact PC Cyborg Corporation for payment. The user was required to send $USD189 to a post office box in Panama.[3] However, this early form of ransomware was relatively unsophisticated and did not spread widely.

One of the most common ways ransomware is delivered is through phishing emails, which contain a link or attachment that, when clicked, will download the malware to the victim's computer. The malware then encrypts the victim's files and displays a message on the screen demanding a ransom. Another way is through the exploitation of vulnerabilities in software and systems, which enable the ransomware to gain access to the network and encrypt files.

It wasn't until the early 2000's that ransomware began to gain momentum as a tactic used by cyber criminals. The "Gpcode" malware, which emerged in 2006 – using the RSA algorithm to create a 56-bit key – was one of the first examples of ransomware to use strong encryption.[4] In the following years, ransomware evolved to become more sophisticated and efficient, with the use of ransomware-as-a-service (RaaS) platforms, and the ability to encrypt network drives and cloud storage.

In the 2010s, ransomware began to gain significant attention as a major threat to organisations, with several high-profile attacks such as CryptoLocker, WannaCry, and Petya/NotPetya causing significant damage and disruption. These attacks highlighted the importance of incident responders and the importance of having incident response plans and procedures in place.

In recent years, ransomware has become one of the most significant cyber threats facing organisations and individuals, with the number of ransomware attacks increasing dramatically. This rising number and increased sophistication has added to the stress felt by incident responders. Ransomware continues to be a major threat in today's digital landscape, with an increasing number of attacks targeting small and medium-sized businesses and individuals.

Ransomware may be classified into three types of attack which are propagated via email phishing, malvertising, exploit kits, and watering hole attacks:[5]

1. Encrypting ransomware: This type of ransomware encrypts victim's files and demands payment in exchange for the decryption key. The authors note that some of the most common variants of

encrypting ransomware include WannaCry, Petya, and Locky.

2. Non-encrypting ransomware: This type of ransomware threatens to publish or delete victim's data unless payment is made. The authors note that this type of ransomware is less common than encrypting ransomware, but can still be highly effective.

3. Hybrid ransomware: This type of ransomware combines features of both encrypting and non-encrypting ransomware. The authors note that this type of ransomware is less common than the other two categories, but can be highly sophisticated and difficult to detect.

There are several stages of a ransomware attack:

1. Initial infection: The attacker uses a variety of tactics to gain initial access to a target's network, such as phishing emails or exploiting vulnerabilities in software.

2. Propagation: Once the attacker has access to one computer, they may try to spread the ransomware to other systems on the network.

3. Encryption: The ransomware will encrypt files on the infected computers, making them inaccessible to the victims.

4. Demands: The attacker will then demand a ransom payment, typically in the form of Bitcoin (or some other type of cryptocurrency), in exchange for a decryption key that will allow the victims to regain access to their files.

5. Payment: If the victim decides to pay the ransom, they will be provided with a decryption key to unlock their files. However, there is no guarantee that the attacker will provide a working key.

6. Recovery: Whether the ransom is paid, the victim will need to take steps to remove the ransomware from their systems and restore any encrypted files from backups.

There are an interesting variety of statistics, mainly from cyber security consultancies, product and services companies surrounding the extent and damage caused by ransomware. For example:

- Businesses lose an average of $140,000 per ransomware attack due to data loss, downtime, and recovery costs. Data loss can cause a business to be down for 10 days or longer, meaning factors such as product sales and business productivity are affected. Businesses who experience ransomware attacks and who pay ransom for their data back, only receive around 60% of their data back.[6]

- There has been an 82% increase in ransomware-related data leaks in 2021, with 2,686 attacks as of Dec. 31, 2021, compared to 1,474 in 2020. With adversaries will continuing to react and move operations to new approaches or malware wherever possible, demonstrating that the ever-adaptable adversary remains the key threat within the cybercrime landscape.[7]

- Ransomware attacks increased by 80% year over year, with the manufacturing industry being the most targeted vertical in 2020.[8]

- Ransomware will cost its victims more around $265 billion (USD) annually by 2031, with a new attack (on a consumer or business) every 2 seconds.[9]

As technology continues to advance, it is likely criminals will continue to pivot in their deployment of ransomware, including:

1. Increased targeting of critical infrastructure: As ransomware attacks become more sophisticated and better funded, it is likely that they will begin to target critical infrastructure such as power grids, transportation systems, and hospitals. These attacks have the potential to cause significant disruption to essential services and could have a severe impact on public safety. There have been several recent high-profile ransomware attacks on critical infrastructure:

    a) In May 2021, the Colonial Pipeline, which supplies 45% of the fuel consumed on the U.S. East Coast, was hit by a ransomware attack. The attackers, believed to be affiliated with the DarkSide ransomware group, demanded a ransom of $4.4 million in Bitcoin. The attack led to fuel shortages and price spikes, and Colonial Pipeline ultimately paid the ransom to regain control of its systems.[10]

    b) In June 2021, JBS, the world's largest meat processing company, was hit by a ransomware attack that disrupted Its operations in the United States, Australia, and Canada. The attackers, believed to be affiliated with the Russian-speaking REvil ransomware group, demanded a ransom of $11 million in Bitcoin. JBS ultimately paid the ransom to restore its systems.[11]

c) In July 2021, the Florida-based software firm Kaseya was hit by a ransomware attack that affected up to 1,500 businesses worldwide. The attackers, believed to be affiliated with the REvil ransomware group, demanded a ransom of $70 million in Bitcoin. The attack exploited a vulnerability in Kaseya's remote management software, allowing the attackers to distribute ransomware to the company's clients.[12]

2. Greater use of double extortion: A trend that has emerged in the ransomware landscape is the use of double extortion, in which attackers not only encrypt the victim's files but also steal sensitive data and threaten to release it if the ransom is not paid. This increases the pressure on victims to pay the ransom and puts their sensitive data at risk. For example:

a) In March 2021, the Taiwanese computer manufacturer Acer was hit by a double extortion ransomware attack. The attackers, believed to be affiliated with the REvil ransomware group, stole financial and personal data before encrypting the company's systems and demanding a ransom of $50 million in Bitcoin (though Acer offered to pay $10 million, which was rejected by the attackers). It is unclear if Acer paid the ransom or not.[13]

3. More use of AI and machine learning: As attackers continue to develop more advanced techniques, it is likely that they will begin to use artificial intelligence

and machine learning to improve the effectiveness of their attacks. This could include using AI to evade detection and target specific victims, as well as to automate the ransomware deployment and demand for payment. For example:

a) In 2018, IBM Research created a proof-of-concept ransomware called DeepLocker, which uses AI to evade detection. DeepLocker uses a neural network to identify its target and only deploys its payload once it has reached the target's device. This makes it difficult for security software to detect and stop the attack.[14]

b) In 2020, a new ransomware variant called LeChiffre was discovered that uses machine learning to target specific files for encryption. LeChiffre's ML algorithm is trained to identify files with sensitive information, such as those containing words like "confidential" or "password."[15]

c) In 2021, researchers from NVIDIA and Boos Allen Hamilton demonstrated how generative adversarial networks (GANs) could be used to create fake images that could fool anti-ransomware tools. The researchers showed that it was possible to create GAN-generated images that looked like legitimate files, but which contained malicious code that could be used to infect a target's computer.[16]

4. Ransomware-as-a-service: Attackers using affiliate networks to distribute ransomware on a wide scale, allowing hackers who are experts in breaching

networks to share profits with the most advanced ransomware groups. For example:

a) GandCrab was a highly successful RaaS ransomware that was active from early 2018 to mid-2019. The GandCrab operators would sell access to the ransomware on underground forums, taking a cut of the ransom payments. At its peak, GandCrab was responsible for as much as 40% of all ransomware attacks, with its authors claiming to have brought in over $2 billion in illicit ransom payments.[17]

b) REvil, also known as Sodinokibi, is another RaaS ransomware that has been active since 2019. The REvil operators provide the ransomware to other attackers through an affiliate program, taking a percentage of the ransom payments. REvil has been responsible for several high-profile attacks, including the JBS and Kaseya attacks in 2021.[18]

c) DarkSide is a RaaS ransomware that gained notoriety after the Colonial Pipeline attack in May 2021. The DarkSide operators provided the ransomware to other attackers through an affiliate program, taking a cut of the ransom payments. Following the Colonial Pipeline attack, the DarkSide operators announced that they were shutting down their operation, but it is unclear if they have actually stopped their activities.[19]

5. More focus on cloud-based environments: With the increasing number of organisations moving their data and applications to the cloud, it is likely that attackers will begin to focus more on cloud-based environments as a means of delivering ransomware. This could include targeting cloud-based file storage systems such as Dropbox and Google Drive, as well as cloud-based applications such as Office 365.

    a) In 2020, Blackbaud, a cloud-based software company that provides fundraising and marketing software to non-profit organisations, was hit by a ransomware attack. The attackers were able to access and steal data from Blackbaud's cloud-based systems, including sensitive information belonging to its clients.[20]

    b) In October 2020, Sopra Steria, a French IT services company, was hit by a ransomware attack that affected its cloud-based infrastructure. The attackers were able to encrypt data on Sopra Steria's cloud-based systems and demanded a ransom of €50 million in Bitcoin.[21]

    c) In April 2020, Cognisant, a global IT services provider, was hit by a ransomware attack that affected its cloud-based systems. The attackers – the Maze ransomware group – encrypted data on Cognisant's systems and demanded a ransom of $50 million.[22]

Defending Against Ransomware

Defending against ransomware involves implementing competent security measures and seeking to prevent the loss of valuable data, financial losses, as well as maintaining reputation and trust with customers, stakeholders and government.

Incident responders, who are responsible for assessing and containing the incident, as well as restoring normal operations, are often under significant psychological strain during these incidents. Factors such as time pressure, uncertainty, and the potential for data loss or reputational damage can influence the psychological well-being and decision-making of incident responders. However, there is still a gap in understanding how these factors affect the outcome of the incident.

Control mechanisms against ransomware attacks include:

1. Backup and recovery can be highly effective in recovering from a ransomware attack, as it allows victims to restore their data to a previous state.

2. Network segmentation can be effective in containing the spread of ransomware, as it limits the attack surface and prevents lateral movement.

3. User education on how to recognise and avoid phishing emails can be effective in preventing ransomware attacks.

4. Anti-malware software to detect and block ransomware attacks, but that it should be regularly updated to stay effective against new variants of ransomware.

A study[23] into ransomware responses proposes a framework for evaluating ransomware response strategies based on four key factors:

1. Ransomware attack attributes: This identified key attributes of ransomware attacks that can impact the effectiveness of response strategies: attack severity, attack speed, attack persistence, and attack complexity.

2. Response objectives: This identified key response objectives that should guide the selection of response strategies: containment, recovery, and prevention.

3. Response strategies: This identified key response strategies that can be used to achieve the response objectives: isolation, backup and recovery, deception, and attack mitigation.

4. Evaluation criteria: This identified key evaluation criteria that can be used to assess the effectiveness of response strategies: response time, data recovery, data loss, and attacker disruption.

Using this framework, the authors evaluated the effectiveness of several ransomware response strategies. Their evaluation focused on two key ransomware variants WannaCry and Locky.

The authors found that:

1. Isolation strategies are most effective for containing ransomware attacks, particularly for WannaCry, which spreads quickly and aggressively. Isolation strategies involve disconnecting infected systems

from the network to prevent further spread of the ransomware.

2. Backup and recovery strategies are most effective for recovering from ransomware attacks, particularly for Locky, which is more persistent and difficult to remove. Backup and recovery strategies involve restoring data from backups that were created prior to the attack.

3. Deception strategies can be effective in disrupting ransomware attacks, but they require a significant amount of resources and planning to implement. Deception strategies involve creating fake files or systems to deceive the attacker into thinking they have successfully encrypted or compromised the victim's data.

4. Attack mitigation strategies, such as anti-malware software and intrusion detection systems, can be effective in preventing ransomware attacks from occurring in the first place. However, these strategies are less effective against new and evolving ransomware variants.

Data Breaches

Like ransomware, and sometimes in tandem, data breaches are an international hot topic. A data breach refers to an incident where unauthorised individuals gain access to sensitive or confidential data held by an organisation, resulting in its exposure, theft, or compromise. It occurs when the security defences of a system or network are breached, allowing cyber criminals to access and exploit valuable information.

During a data breach, attackers typically exploit vulnerabilities in an organisation's infrastructure, such as weak passwords, unpatched software, or social engineering techniques, to gain unauthorised access. Once inside the network, they may exfiltrate data, modify it, or cause other forms of damage.

Data breaches have been a persistent and evolving threat throughout the history of computer and network technology. Early data breaches primarily involved hacking into computer systems to gain unauthorised access to sensitive information.

The 2000s saw a significant increase in data breaches, driven by the growing reliance on digital systems and the internet. The AOL Time Warner Data Breach in 2005, where a former employee stole and sold 92 million AOL customer email addresses, highlighted the potential impact of insider threats. In 2007 TJX suffered a significant security breach where cyber criminals gained unauthorised access resulting In the theft of millions of customer credit card numbers and personal information.

Other significant data breaches have included the Sony PlayStation Network breach in 2011 compromised the personal information of over 77 million users; The Target data breach in 2013 which exposed the credit card information of 41 million customers and resulted in significant financial and reputational losses for the company; and the Yahoo data breaches in 2013 and 2014, affecting billions of user accounts, were among the largest breaches in history.

More recent data breaches have included the Ashley Madison breach, where the personal information of millions of users was leaked; and the U.S Government Office of Personnel Management breach, which exposed sensitive data of millions of federal employees.

Ransomware attacks, where attackers encrypt an organisation's data and demand a ransom for its release, became increasingly prevalent in recent years, with notable incidents such as the WannaCry and NotPetya attacks in 2017.

As technology continues to advance, the complexity and frequency of data breaches have increased. The motivations behind data breaches have expanded beyond financial gain to include espionage, activism, and disruption.

A data breach may involve several stages as attackers navigate their way through an organisation's systems and infrastructure. While the specifics can vary, the following stages provide a general overview:

1. Reconnaissance: In this initial stage, attackers gather information about the target organisation. This may involve conducting online research, scanning for vulnerabilities, and identifying potential entry points

or weaknesses in the organisation's defences. Attackers may also gather intelligence about employees, systems, and security protocols.

2. Initial Compromise: Once attackers have identified potential vulnerabilities, they exploit them to gain an initial foothold in the target organisation's network. This could involve various methods, such as phishing emails, social engineering, exploiting software vulnerabilities, or compromising weak credentials. The goal is to establish an entry point for further access and exploration.

3. Lateral Movement: After gaining initial access, attackers aim to explore and expand their presence within the organisation's network. They move laterally, seeking out valuable data, sensitive systems, or administrative privileges. This stage involves compromising additional machines or accounts, exploiting trust relationships, and searching for high-value targets within the network.

4. Data Collection: At this stage, attackers locate and exfiltrate valuable data from the compromised systems. They may target PII, financial data, intellectual property, or other sensitive information that holds value to them or potential buyers. Data can be exfiltrated through various techniques, such as copying files to remote servers, using covert channels, or hiding within seemingly innocuous network traffic.

5. Persistence and Cover-Up: To maintain access and avoid detection, attackers employ various techniques to ensure their continued presence within the

compromised systems. This may involve creating backdoors, establishing remote access capabilities, or modifying system configurations to maintain persistence. They also attempt to cover their tracks by deleting logs, altering timestamps, or obfuscating their activities to make it challenging for defenders to identify the breach.

Data breaches can have severe consequences for organisations, including:

1. Loss of Sensitive Information: Attackers may gain access to personally identifiable information, financial data, trade secrets, intellectual property, or other sensitive information. The exposure of this data can lead to identity theft, financial fraud, reputational damage, or competitive disadvantage.

2. Legal and Regulatory Consequences: Depending on the jurisdiction and industry, organisations may be subject to various legal and regulatory obligations regarding the protection of customer data. A data breach can result in legal actions, fines, and penalties for non-compliance with data protection regulations, such as the Australian Notifiable Data Breach Scheme, the European Union General Data Protection Regulation (GDPR) or the California Consumer Privacy Act.

3. Financial Loss: Data breaches can lead to significant financial losses for organisations. This includes expenses associated with incident response, forensic investigations, customer notifications, legal fees, potential lawsuits, and the costs of implementing

enhanced security measures to prevent future breaches.

4. Reputational Damage: When customer data is compromised, organisations often suffer reputational damage and loss of customer trust. The negative publicity surrounding a data breach may lead to customer churn, decreased revenue, and long-term damage to the brand's reputation.

5. Operational Disruption: Data breaches can disrupt business operations, especially if critical systems or networks are compromised or encrypted with ransomware. This can result in downtime, loss of productivity, and the need for extensive recovery efforts to restore normal operations.

6. Exploitation or Extortion: In some cases, attackers exploit the compromised data or leverage their access for financial gain. This could involve selling the stolen data on the black market, using it for identity theft or fraud, conducting insider trading, or engaging in other criminal activities. Alternatively, attackers may opt for extortion, deploying ransomware or threatening to expose the stolen data unless a ransom is paid.

While a data breach and a ransomware attack can occur independently, nowadays they are often interconnected. Attackers may gain unauthorised access to an organisation's systems, exfiltrate sensitive data, and then deploy ransomware to encrypt the stolen data or threaten its public release if the ransom is not paid. This combination of data breach and ransomware attack adds a significant element of coercion and urgency to the situation.

In recent years, ransomware attacks have become increasingly prevalent and sophisticated. Attackers often target organisations with valuable data or critical operations, such as healthcare institutions, financial organisations, or government agencies. The potential consequences of a successful ransomware attack include financial loss, operational disruption, reputational damage, and potential data exposure if the ransom is not paid or the attackers decide to publicly release the stolen information.

Globally, the first quarter of 2023 saw more than six million data records exposed through data breaches,[24] whilst the global average cost of a data breach in 2023 was USD 4.45 million, a 15% increase over 3 years.[25] In Australia, most data breaches (88%) involved the personal information of 5,000 or fewer individuals worldwide. Breaches affecting 100 or fewer individuals comprised 62% of notifications and breaches affecting between 1 and 10 individuals accounted for 43% of notifications.[26]

Predicting the future of criminal activity with respect to data breaches is challenging, as cyber criminals continually adapt their tactics and techniques. However, several trends and possibilities can be considered, which incident responders – and those who ply their trade in threat-intelligence – should consider, including:

1. Increased sophistication as cyber criminals develop more complex methods for conducting data breaches, for example the use of advanced malware, AI techniques, automation, and encryption techniques to evade detection and enhance the effectiveness of their attacks.

2. Targeting emerging technologies such as Internet of Things, cloud computing, and artificial intelligence, cyber criminals may shift their focus to exploit vulnerabilities in these technologies. They may target interconnected devices, cloud storage systems, and AI algorithms to gain unauthorised access, disrupt services, or manipulate data.

3. Insider threats, where employees or insiders intentionally or unintentionally compromise data security, will continue to pose a risk. Cyber criminals may exploit insider access, social engineering, or collusion with employees to gain unauthorised access to sensitive data.

4. State-sponsored cyber attacks for political, economic, or espionage purposes, where nation-states engage in large-scale data breaches to steal intellectual property, disrupt critical infrastructure, or conduct espionage on other countries.

5. Cyber criminals may further organise themselves into criminal networks, offering hacking tools, services, and expertise on the dark web. This "cybercrime-as-a-service" model may lead to an increase in the number of actors involved in data breaches, making it more difficult to trace and attribute attacks.

6. With the increasing emphasis on data privacy and protection, governments and regulatory bodies are likely to introduce stricter regulations and enforcement mechanisms. This may (or may not) deter some criminal activities and encourage organisations to enhance their security measures.

Defending Against Data Breaches

Defending against data breaches requires competence, planning and execution. As the saying goes, an ounce of prevention is better than a pound of cure. Organisations can implement numerous proactive measures to defend against data breaches and strengthen their overall cyber security posture, including:

1. Educating employees about cyber security best practices, such as recognising phishing emails, using strong passwords, and avoiding suspicious downloads or websites. Regular training sessions and awareness campaigns can help create a security-conscious culture within the organisation.

2. Implementation of strong authentication mechanisms, such as multi-factor authentication, to protect user accounts. Apply the principle of least privilege, granting users only the permissions necessary to perform their duties. Regularly review and revoke unnecessary privileges to limit potential attack surfaces.

3. Divide the network into distinct segments, using firewalls and access controls, to restrict lateral movement in case of a breach. This limits the impact of an attacker's access and helps contain the breach within a specific segment.

4. Keep all software, including operating systems, applications, and firmware, up to date with the latest security patches. Regularly apply updates to address known vulnerabilities and protect against exploitation.

5. Deploy firewalls, intrusion detection and prevention systems, and secure web gateways to monitor and control network traffic. These tools help detect and block malicious activities, such as unauthorised access attempts or malware downloads, at the network perimeter.

6. Install and maintain endpoint security solutions, including antivirus and anti-malware software, on all devices. Use advanced endpoint detection and response solutions to identify and respond to threats in real-time.

7. Utilise encryption to protect sensitive data both in transit and at rest. This includes encrypting communication channels (e.g., HTTPS) and utilising encryption technologies, such as full-disk encryption or database encryption, to protect data stored on devices and servers.

8. Perform regular backups of critical data and test the restore process to ensure data integrity and availability. Backups can help recover data in the event of a breach, ransomware attack, or system failure.

9. Develop an incident response plan that outlines the steps to be taken in the event of a data breach. This plan should include procedures for containment, investigation, notification, and recovery. Regularly test and update the plan to ensure its effectiveness.

10. Implement a comprehensive monitoring system to detect anomalous activities and potential indicators of compromise. Use threat intelligence sources to

stay informed about emerging threats and vulnerabilities relevant to the organisation.

11. Assess and manage the cyber security posture of third-party vendors and partners. Ensure they have appropriate security controls in place when accessing or processing sensitive data on behalf of the organisation.

12. Conduct regular security assessments, including vulnerability scanning, penetration testing, and security audits, to identify weaknesses and address them proactively.

By adopting a layered approach to cyber security, organisations can significantly enhance their defences against data breaches. It is crucial to regularly review and update security measures, staying abreast of the evolving threat landscape, and adapting security strategies accordingly. Considerations include:

1. Importance of defence strategies which play a crucial role in mitigating the impact of breaches and protecting sensitive information. Effective defence strategies involve a combination of technical controls, organisational policies, and proactive incident response planning.

2. Proactive measures such as access controls, encryption, intrusion detection systems, and incident response planning are essential for defending against data breaches. Implementing these measures can help prevent unauthorised access, detect suspicious activities, and respond promptly to incidents.

3. Threat assessment and risk management to understand the potential losses from data breaches, evaluating the costs of cyber security measures, and prioritising investments accordingly can enhance breach prevention.

4. Information systems control activities such as security policies, incident response planning, monitoring, and employee training, contribute to preventing and mitigating data breaches. Effectively implementing and maintaining these control activities is essential for a strong defence posture.

5. Post-breach control activities where following a data breach, organisations focus on post-breach control activities, including incident response, investigation, and remediation. These activities help organisations learn from breaches, strengthen their defence mechanisms, and prevent future incidents.

6. Continuous improvement as data breach defence is an ongoing process that requires continuous improvement. Regularly evaluating the effectiveness of defence strategies, staying updated on emerging threats, and adapting security measures accordingly contribute to a robust defence posture.

Research[27] has demonstrated the importance of adopting a multifaceted strategic approach to fortify defences against data breaches. Such an approach should involve the amalgamation of proactive security measures, including encryption, access controls, and comprehensive employee training programs.

Furthermore, the research underscores the challenges associated with the timely detection of data breaches. The study highlights the persistence of advanced persistent threats and other highly sophisticated attack vectors, which often evade detection for extended durations. Consequently, the research advocates for continuous monitoring and robust anomaly detection mechanisms as fundamental components of a proactive security posture.

A central theme elucidated by the study revolves around the human element within the data breach defence paradigm. Employee training and awareness programs are acknowledged as pivotal tools in mitigating insider threats and inadvertent data exposure. Simultaneously, encryption emerges as a cornerstone of data security, both at rest and in transit.

The research further accentuates the crucial role played by well-defined incident response plans, which delineate precise steps for breach containment and mitigation. These comprehensive plans encompass strategies for effective communication with affected stakeholders and regulatory authorities.

In addition, the research underscores the escalating risks posed by third-party entities and partners. The study recommends rigorous evaluation of the security practices and data handling procedures of such entities to mitigate potential vulnerabilities.

Lastly, the authors recognises the significance of regulatory compliance in the context of data breach defence. It emphasises the need for adherence to stringent data protection regulations, such as GDPR, given the severe financial and reputational consequences associated with non-compliance.

Additional research[28] addresses the critical issue of data breach prevention by introducing a systematic framework that combines threat assessment and optimal investments in cyber security. The authors employ a quantitative approach, utilising a stochastic model that incorporates key parameters such as threat likelihood, vulnerability, and the potential impact of a data breach. The authors developed a dynamic programming model to determine the optimal allocation of resources for cyber security investments, emphasising the trade-offs between enhancing security and minimising operational costs.

A noteworthy aspect of their research is the incorporation of a threat assessment component that quantifies the evolving threat landscape. By evaluating the likelihood of specific threats, organisations can make informed decisions regarding cyber security investments. The study also underscores the importance of continuously updating threat assessments to adapt to the ever-changing nature of cyber threats.

Furthermore, the authors offer practical recommendations for organisations seeking to enhance their cyber security posture. They propose a risk-based approach that allocates resources based on the criticality of data assets and potential losses in the event of a breach. This approach aligns cyber security investments with an organisation's strategic objectives and risk tolerance.

This research provides a robust framework that integrates threat assessment and optimal cyber security investments. Their quantitative model assists organisations in making informed decisions to prevent data breaches effectively, emphasising the dynamic nature of the cyber threat landscape and the importance of aligning cyber security strategies with organisational risk profiles.

Further research[29] explores the strategies and complexities involved in preventing and responding to data breaches. The authors underscore the pervasive nature of data breaches and their far-reaching consequences. The research highlights the need for adaptable, proactive, and multi-faceted approaches to data breach protection.

The research delineates key strategies, including encryption, access controls, employee training, and incident response planning, all integral to safeguarding against data breaches. Encryption is recognised as a fundamental security measure, while access controls restrict unauthorised access. Employee training and awareness programs are acknowledged for their role in mitigating insider threats, and incident response planning is deemed critical for effective breach containment and remediation.

Despite these strategies, the authors discuss the intricate challenges posed by data breaches. Timely breach detection, especially for advanced threats, remains a significant hurdle, along with the evolving tactics of cyber criminals, third-party risks, and regulatory compliance further complicate the landscape.

The study concludes by advocating a proactive, risk-based approach that aligns breach protection strategies with an organisation's risk profile and critical data assets. The authors emphasise the importance of continuous threat assessment and adaptive security measures.

More research[30] delves into the realm of data security breaches and their repercussions on information systems control activities. This study investigates the dynamic interplay between security breaches and subsequent control measures adopted by organisations.

The authors commence by acknowledging the growing frequency and severity of data security breaches across various sectors, underscoring their potential for significant financial losses and damage to an organisation's reputation. This study concentrates on the post-breach scenario, providing insights into how organisations respond to such incidents.

Central to the research is the investigation of control activities implemented by organisations following a data breach. It reveals that organisations tend to enhance their control environments in the wake of a breach. These post-breach control activities span various domains, including access controls, security policies, and monitoring mechanisms. The study emphasises that while organisations bolster their control activities, the effectiveness of these measures depends on factors such as the breach's severity and regulatory implications.

Furthermore, the study illuminates the role of audit committees and internal auditors in post-breach control activities, highlighting the significance of these stakeholders in ensuring the adequacy of control activities and adherence to compliance requirements.

Denial of Service

A Denial of Service (DoS) attack is a malicious act that aims to disrupt the availability of a computer system, network, or online service, making it inaccessible to its intended users. The primary goal of a DoS attack is to overwhelm the targeted system's resources, such as bandwidth, processing power, or memory, rendering it incapable of handling legitimate requests.

In a DoS attack, the attacker typically floods the target system with a high volume of requests or malicious traffic. This excessive load consumes the system's resources and prevents it from servicing legitimate users or clients. As a result, the system becomes slow, unresponsive, or completely inaccessible, leading to a denial of service to legitimate users.

DoS attacks have a long history that dates to the early days of the internet. The term "Denial of Service" was first used in the early 1990s to describe attacks that aimed to make a network or service unavailable to its intended users. In 1996, a significant DoS attack occurred when a hacker named Timothy C. Lloyd launched a series of attacks targeting internet service providers, including AOL and Netcom. These attacks caused service disruptions for millions of users.

In the early 2000s, DoS attacks continued to evolve and gain attention as the internet became more integral to businesses and individuals. The "Ping of Death" attack was a notable DoS attack that exploited vulnerabilities in certain operating systems by sending oversized or malformed packets, causing system crashes or freezes. DoS attacks then progressed to Distributed Denial of Service (DDoS) attacks which involve multiple compromised computers (known as botnets) flooding a target with a massive volume of traffic, overwhelming its resources and causing service disruptions. For example, the Mafiaboy case in 2000 involved a 15-year-old Canadian hacker who launched DDoS attacks against major websites, including Yahoo!, Amazon, and eBay, resulting in significant downtime.

DDoS attacks evolved, driven by the increasing availability of botnets and the growth of IoT devices. This was highlighted by the Mirai botnet in 2016, which infected insecure IoT devices and was responsible for launching massive DDoS attacks against various targets, including DNS service provider Dyn, resulting in widespread service outages.

DDoS attacks then became a favoured tool for hacktivist groups and cyber criminals, with motivations ranging from ideological reasons to extortion attempts against targeted organisations.

DDoS attacks continue to be a prevalent and evolving threat. Attackers employ various techniques, such as amplification attacks (using vulnerable servers to amplify attack traffic) and application-layer attacks (targeting specific vulnerabilities in applications). The scale and complexity of DDoS attacks have increased, with attackers utilising botnets with vast computational power and employing advanced evasion techniques to bypass mitigation measures.

There are various types of DoS attacks, including:

1. Flood attacks which overwhelm the target system with a flood of data packets or requests. For example, a TCP/IP-based SYN flood attack exploits the handshake process, sending numerous

connection requests without completing the handshake, exhausting the system's resources.

2. Amplification attacks where an attacker sends a small request to a vulnerable system that responds with a significantly larger reply. By spoofing the source IP address, the attacker can amplify the traffic directed at the target, causing a significant increase in data volume that overwhelms the system.

3. Application-layer attacks which exploit vulnerabilities in the target application or service. For instance, a HTTP flood attack sends a high volume of seemingly legitimate HTTP requests, overwhelming the web server and affecting its ability to process valid requests.

4. DDoS attacks which involve multiple compromised devices, forming a botnet or a network of controlled systems. The attacker orchestrates the attack by coordinating the compromised devices to flood the target with traffic simultaneously, amplifying the impact and making it harder to mitigate.

The motivations behind DoS and DDoS attacks can vary. They may be carried out to disrupt services, extort money from targeted organisations, exact revenge, demonstrate technical prowess, or even act as a diversionary tactic to divert attention from other malicious activities. DoS attacks can have significant consequences for organisations that fall victim to them, including:

1. Service disruption or downtime where the targeted organisation's website, online services, or network infrastructure may become inaccessible to legitimate

users, resulting in loss of productivity, revenue, and customer trust.

2.   Downtime and service disruption which can lead to financial losses for organisations, for example if the attack prevents customers from accessing e-commerce platforms or conducting transactions, it may impact revenue generation.

3.   Harm an organisation's reputation or erosion of customer trust. Customers may perceive the organisation as unreliable, leading to a loss of business opportunities and customer loyalty. Negative publicity and media attention can further damage the organisation's reputation, impacting its long-term viability.

4.   An inability to access services can frustrate and disappoint customers, leading to dissatisfaction. If customers experience repeated or prolonged disruptions, they may seek alternative service providers, resulting in customer churn and a decline in market share.

5.   Depending on the nature of the organisation and the industry it operates in, a DoS attack may have legal and compliance implications. For example, organisations handling sensitive customer data, such as financial institutions or healthcare providers, may face legal repercussions if the attack results in unauthorised access to or disclosure of confidential information.

6.   Requiring significant resources and effort with incident response teams investigating the attack, mitigating its impact, and restoring normal

operations. This diverts attention from regular business activities and places a strain on the organisation's resources, both in terms of personnel and finances.

7. In some cases, the consequences of a DoS attack can extend beyond the immediate incident. Organisations may face increased scrutiny from customers, partners, and regulators, making it harder to regain trust and rebuild relationships. This long-term damage can hinder future growth and business opportunities.

The severity of these consequences can vary depending on the duration, scale, and nature of the DoS attack, as well as the organisation's preparedness and response capabilities. Implementing robust security measures and having incident response plans in place can help mitigate the impact of such attacks.

Defending Against a Denial of Service Attack

Defending against DoS attacks requires a multi-layered approach that combines proactive measures, network security controls, and incident response planning, including:

1. Engage with a reputable DoS mitigation service provider. These services employ advanced traffic monitoring and filtering techniques to detect and mitigate volumetric, application-layer, and protocol-based attacks. They can help absorb and filter out malicious traffic before it reaches a network.

2. Implement network traffic monitoring tools and intrusion detection systems to identify unusual patterns or traffic spikes that may indicate a DoS attack in progress. Anomaly detection algorithms can help detect deviations from normal network behaviour and trigger alerts.

3. Distribute network traffic across multiple servers or data centres using load balancing techniques. This approach helps distribute the load and prevents a single point of failure. Scalability ensures infrastructure can handle increased traffic during an attack.

4. Configure firewalls, routers, and intrusion prevention systems to filter and block traffic from suspicious or blacklisted IP addresses. Implement rate limiting to restrict the number of requests or connections from a single IP address, preventing overwhelming traffic.

5. Protect web applications against application-layer attacks by implementing secure coding practices, conducting regular vulnerability assessments, and using web application firewalls (WAFs). A WAF can detect and block malicious traffic targeting specific vulnerabilities in your applications.

6. Employ a Content Delivery Network (CDN) service to distribute content geographically, reducing the load on servers and improving resilience against DoS attacks. CDNs can also help absorb and mitigate DDoS attacks by caching and delivering content closer to end-users.

7. Develop a comprehensive incident response plan that includes specific procedures for handling DoS attacks. This plan should outline roles, responsibilities, communication protocols, and steps for mitigating and recovering from an attack. Regularly test and update the plan to ensure its effectiveness.

8. Implement bandwidth management policies to prioritise critical network traffic during an attack. This helps ensure that essential services and applications remain accessible, even under heavy traffic load.

9. Collaboration with ISPs and service providers who may offer specialised services or have protocols in place to mitigate DoS attacks upstream, reducing the impact on your network.

10. Educate employees about DoS attacks, their impact, and the importance of following security best practices. Training should cover identifying phishing attempts, avoiding suspicious downloads, and reporting any unusual network behaviour promptly.

There is no single solution which can eliminate the risk of a DoS attack. Employing a combination of preventive measures, detection systems, and response plans can significantly enhance an organisation's resilience to such attacks. Regular monitoring, testing, and staying informed about emerging attack techniques are also essential for effective defence.

The Survey

This research is bolstered using an anonymous survey distributed to incident responders. 64 participants took place, across a wide range of job types and whilst mostly male, was represented by a wide range of ages and experience. Similarly, there was a wide range of education levels represented.

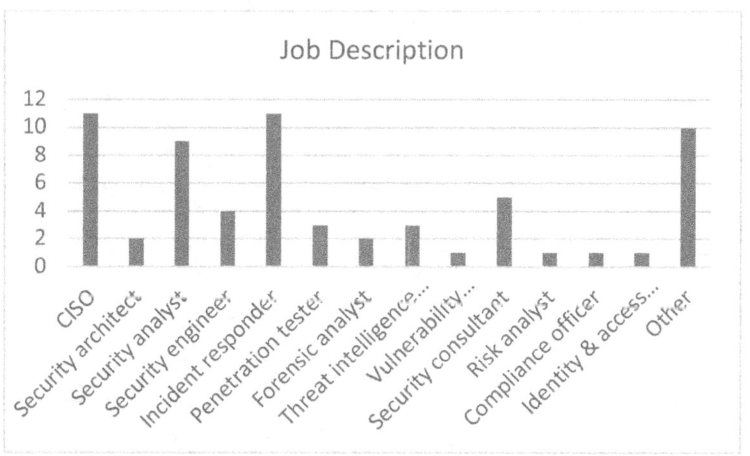

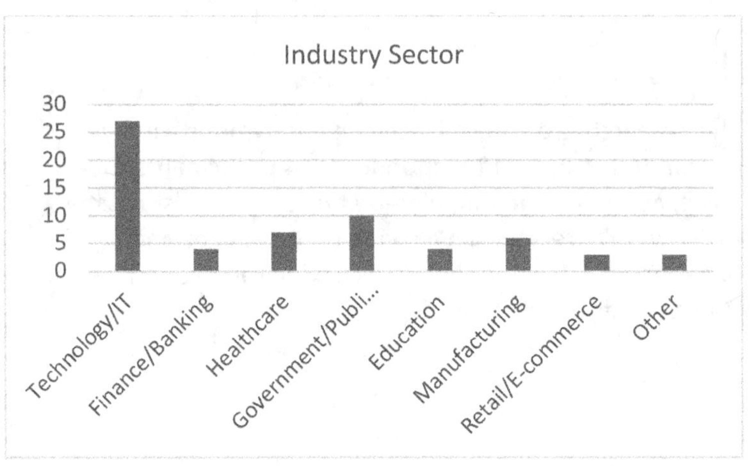

Industry Sector
30
25
20
15
10
5
0
Technology/IT
Finance/Banking
Healthcare
Government/Publi...
Education
Manufacturing
Retail/E-commerce
Other

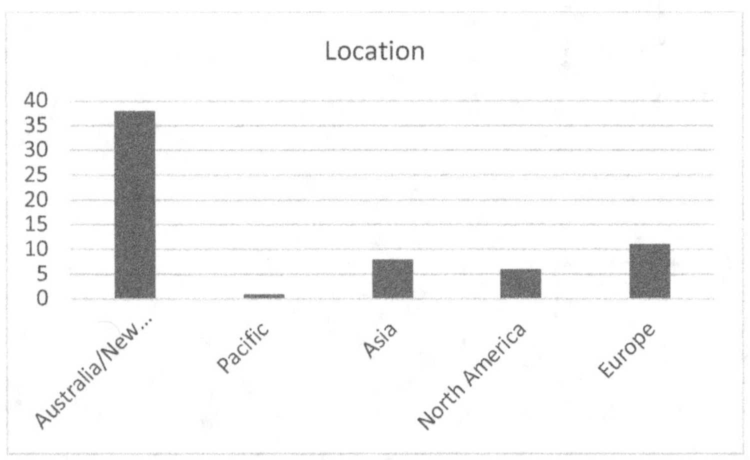

Location
40
35
30
25
20
15
10
5
0
Australia/New...
Pacific
Asia
North America
Europe

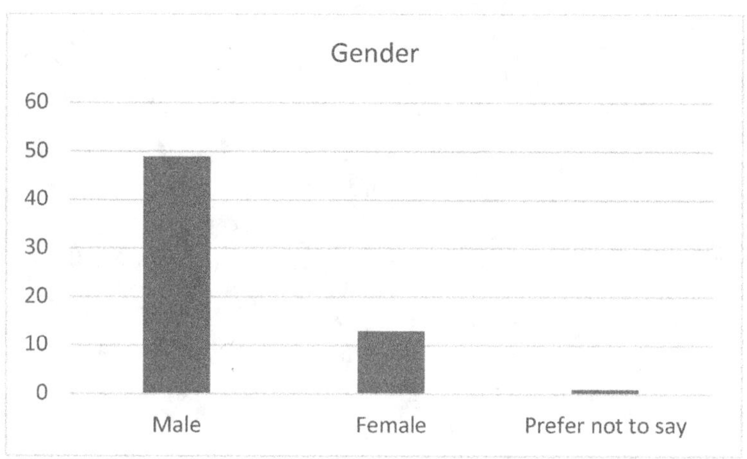

Gender
60
50
40
30
20
10
0
Male
Female
Prefer not to say

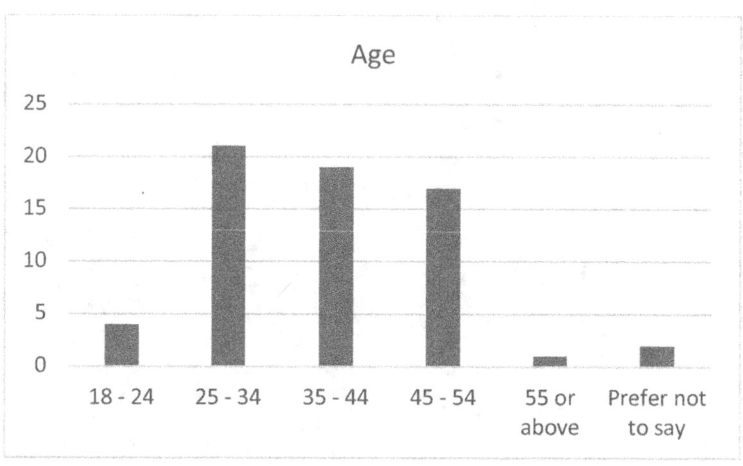

Age
25
20
15
10
5
0
18 - 24
25 - 34
35 - 44
45 - 54
55 or above
Prefer not to say

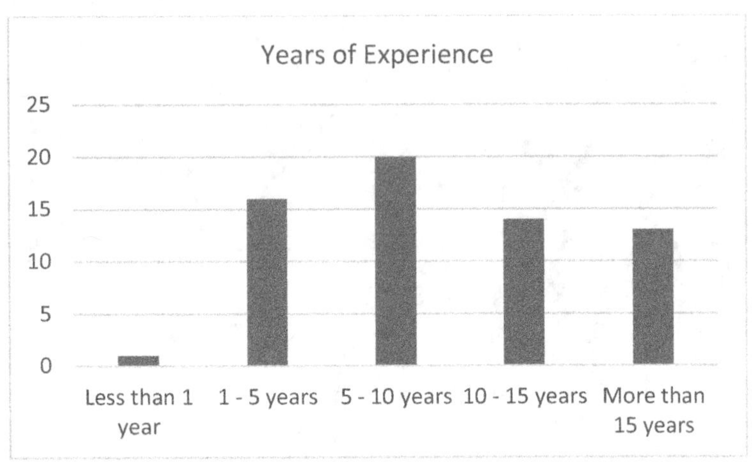
Years of Experience
25
20
15
10
5
0
Less than 1 year
1 - 5 years
5 - 10 years
10 - 15 years
More than 15 years

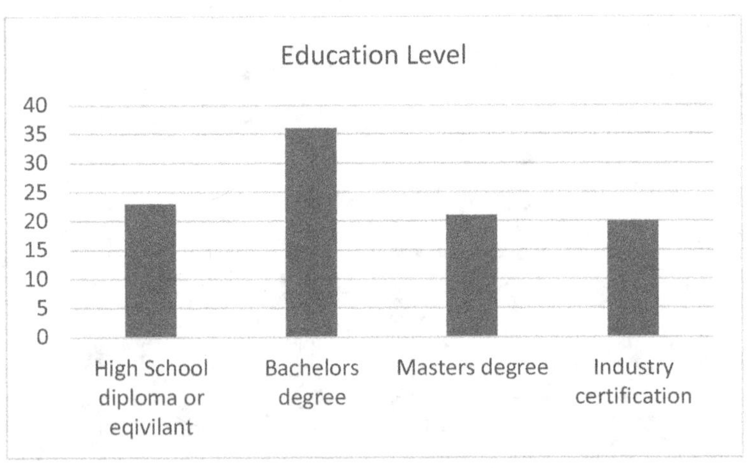
Education Level
40
35
30
25
20
15
10
5
0
High School diploma or eqivilant
Bachelors degree
Masters degree
Industry certification

The median age of ICT Security Specialists in Australia is 39 years, with this survey being representative of 30% in the 35 – 44 age group (though 33% were in the 25 – 24 age group). This is similar to the Australian 'all jobs' average of 40 years. Females make up 14% of the ICT Security Specialists workforce, with this survey being representative of 20%. This is 34 percentage points below the 'all jobs' average of 48%.[31]

40% of Australian ICT Security Specialists hold a Bachelors degree with 23% holding post-graduate qualifications. This survey represents 36% holding a Bachelors degree and 21% holding post-graduate qualifications.[32]

Unsurprisingly, given the subject matter of this publication, Incident Responders, at over 17% (along with CISO's), were the most prominent job title to respond to this survey.

Incident Response

Cyber incident response refers to the process of identifying, containing, and mitigating the impact of a cyber-attack. It is a critical aspect of cyber security that aims to minimise the damage caused by an attack and restore normal operations as quickly as possible. A cyber incident response plan should include procedures for communicating and coordinating with different stakeholders, including internal teams, external partners, and law enforcement agencies. This will help to ensure that all parties are aware of the incident and are working together to contain and resolve it.

The incident response process typically follows a defined lifecycle, which includes the following phases:

1. Preparation: Develop incident response plans and procedures, as well as training incident responders. This includes identifying critical assets and systems, establishing incident response teams, and determining roles and responsibilities.

2. Identification: Identify and confirm the existence of a cyber incident. This may involve analysing network traffic, reviewing system logs, and conducting vulnerability assessments. It is important to have a clear and consistent way to identify and classify different types of incidents, such as data breaches, denial of service attacks, and phishing attempts. This will help to prioritise response efforts and determine the appropriate level of action to take.

3. Containment: Contain the attack and prevent it from spreading. This includes isolating infected systems, disabling compromised accounts, and implementing

firewalls and other security measures. The goal of incident response is to contain the incident and prevent it from spreading. This may involve taking steps such as disconnecting affected systems from the network, shutting down services, and isolating compromised devices. In the case of ransomware, it is also important to identify the specific type of ransomware that is involved, as different variants may have different behaviours and vulnerabilities that can be exploited.

4. Eradication: Identify and remove the cause of the incident. This includes analysing malware and other malicious code, patching vulnerabilities, and restoring systems to a known good state. Eradication is the process of removing the malicious software or code that caused the incident, which can be achieved through various methods such as scanning, patching, and restoring from backups.

5. Recovery: After an incident has been contained and eradicated, the focus shifts to recovery and restoration of normal operations. This may involve restoring systems and data from backups, testing and verifying the integrity of recovered data, and making any necessary changes to security controls to prevent a similar incident from happening in the future. In a ransomware incident, the attackers may have encrypted or otherwise compromised sensitive data, making it difficult or impossible to recover. It is essential to have a data backup and disaster recovery plan in place so that the organisation can restore its operations as soon as possible.

6. Regular training and testing: This will help to ensure all employees are familiar with their roles and responsibilities in the event of a cyber incident. This will also help to identify any gaps or weaknesses in the incident response plan that need to be addressed.

7. Post-incident review: To identify any lessons learned and make any necessary changes to the incident response plan. This will help to improve the overall incident response capabilities and preparedness of the organisation.

A study[33] into the best practices for developing a cyber security response plan identified five key components of an effective ransomware response plan:

1. Pre-incident planning: Identifying critical assets, defining roles and responsibilities, and establishing communication channels and protocols.

2. Detection and analysis: The use of antivirus software, intrusion detection systems, and network monitoring tools to identify and alert on ransomware activity.

3. Containment and eradication: Disconnecting infected systems from the network, removing the ransomware from infected systems, and restoring data from backups.

4. Recovery and remediation: Restoring data from backups, patching vulnerabilities, and implementing additional security controls to prevent future incidents.

5. Post-incident analysis and improvement: Analysing the root cause of the incident, assessing the effectiveness of the response plan, and identifying opportunities for improvement.

The authors also highlight several key best practices for implementing a response plan, including:

1. Regular testing and training of employees on the ransomware response plan to ensure it remains effective and up-to-date.

2. Multi-disciplinary teams in the development and execution of the ransomware response plan, including IT, legal, and management.

3. Communication and coordination between stakeholders during a ransomware incident, including clear escalation paths and decision-making processes.

4. Compliance with regulations and standards such as the NIST Cyber security Framework and the ISO/IEC 27001 standard.

Managing the psychological impact on staff during a cyber-attack can be a critical component of an effective incident response. The following are some key psychological issues to consider when managing staff who are responding to a cyber-attack:

1. Stress and burnout: Responding to a cyber-attack can be a highly stressful and demanding process, and staff may be at risk of experiencing burnout or other negative psychological effects as a result. Responding to a cyber-attack may require round-the-clock work and can involve high levels of pressure to resolve the

issue quickly. This can lead to staff working long hours and neglecting their personal lives. It is important to provide staff with appropriate support and resources to help them manage the stress and maintain their well-being.

2. Trauma: In some cases, staff may experience trauma because of a cyber-attack, particularly if sensitive or personal information has been compromised or if the attack has resulted in significant disruption to operations. Staff involved in responding to a cyber-attack may be exposed to the effects of the attack, such as seeing the damage caused to computer systems or the impact on the organisation's operations. It is important to provide staff with access to appropriate counselling and other mental health resources to help them cope with the trauma.

3. Fear and anxiety: Staff may experience fear and anxiety because of a cyber-attack, particularly if they feel that their personal information or the organisation's data is at risk. Cyber security staff may be working with incomplete information about the attack and its impact, which can lead to uncertainty and anxiety. Responding to a cyber-attack can be a complex process, and staff may be concerned about the possibility of the attack escalating or spreading to other systems. It is important to provide staff with clear and accurate information about the incident and the steps being taken to address it, as well as to provide them with appropriate training and resources to help them understand and manage the risks.

4. Blame and guilt: Staff may feel blame or guilt if they believe they played a role in the cyber-attack or if they feel that they could have done more to prevent it. Cyber security staff may feel that they failed to prevent the attack, even if they were not responsible for the organisation's overall security posture. Staff involved in responding to a cyber-attack may face blame and criticism from others, such as senior management or customers affected by the attack. It is important to provide staff with a clear understanding of their roles and responsibilities during an incident and to communicate that the incident is not their fault.

5. Isolation: Staff may feel isolated during an incident response, particularly if they are working remotely. Cyber security staff may be physically isolated from their colleagues or other support systems, particularly if they are working remotely or outside of normal business hours. Staff may feel that they are not receiving adequate support or resources from their organisation, which can contribute to feelings of isolation and burnout. Additionally, staff may feel that they are unable to share their experiences or feelings with others who are not directly involved in the response. It is important to maintain regular communication and check-ins with staff, and to provide them with opportunities to connect with their colleagues and with incident response team.

6. Fatigue: Cyber incident response can be a long-term and tiring process, and staff may experience fatigue as a result. Responding to a cyber-attack can involve a high volume of work, including analysing data,

coordinating with stakeholders, and implementing security measures, which can contribute to fatigue. Following a cyber-attack, staff may not have adequate time to recover and recharge before returning to normal work responsibilities, which can lead to prolonged fatigue. It is important to provide staff with adequate rest and breaks, and to rotate staff if necessary to ensure that they are not overworked.

When questioned "How would you rate your overall stress level when responding to a cyber security incident?" 41% stated 'moderate', while 28% stated 'high'. When asked "How often do you perceive responding to a cyber security incident as a potential threat to your well-being or safety?" 34% stated 'rarely', whilst responses of 'sometimes' and 'often' were equal at 23%. Troubling, 8% stated 'always'.

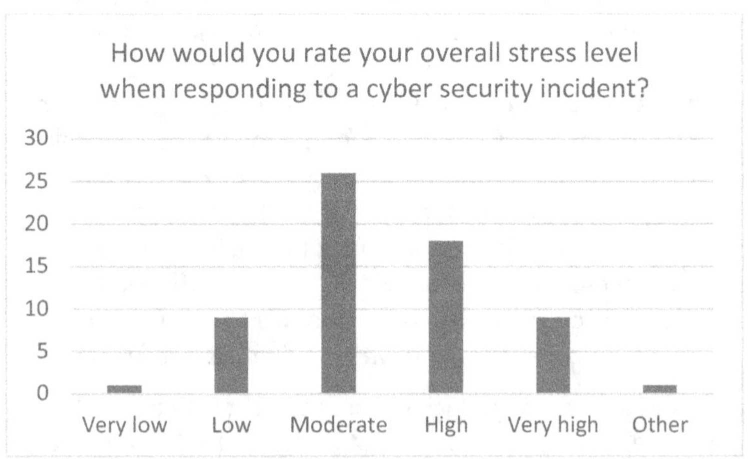

A mechanism for organisations to respond to employee stress and impacts to well-being and safety is the implementation of an Employee Assistance Program (EAP) that provides mental health support to employees during and after the incident. In addition, organisations should ensure that their incident response teams are aware of these issues and are trained to recognise and respond to them.

An EAP is a workplace benefit program that provides employees with confidential counselling and support services to address personal or work-related challenges. EAPs are typically offered by employers as part of an employee benefits package and are designed to help employees manage a range of issues, including mental health concerns, substance abuse, financial difficulties, and relationship problems.

EAPs generally provide short-term counselling services to employees and their family members, typically through phone or in-person sessions with licensed mental health professionals. Some EAPs may also offer additional support services, such as legal or financial counselling, wellness programs, and referrals to community resources.

One of the key benefits of an EAP is that it provides a confidential and non-judgmental space for employees to seek support and guidance for personal or work-related issues. By offering this type of support, employers can help employees manage stress and reduce the impact of personal challenges on their work performance, job satisfaction, and overall well-being.

Whilst there is no specific research conducted within the cyber security industry, research[34] conducted within the teaching sector where an EAP program had been introduced revealed the EAP cost the Department $409.27 per EAP user, or $14.26 per head count employee. Presenteeism – the act of employees being physically present at work but not fully engaged or productive due to illness, stress, or other factors, leading to reduced performance and efficiency – savings was the largest benefit, comprising 88% of the total EAP benefits. Additionally, the EAP produced $96,787 in direct savings in relief teachers, almost the cost of an additional teacher.

Employers may also benefit from offering an EAP by reducing employee turnover, absenteeism, and healthcare costs, as well as promoting a healthier and more productive workforce.

Responding to a Cyber Incident

Cyber security incident response is a process organisations use to assess, respond to, and mitigate cyber threats. It is an essential part of protecting businesses from the dangers of cybercrime. A cyber incident response plan is a documented set of instructions that help businesses quickly and efficiently detect cyber attacks, isolate any affected system, or network, and recover from the resultant loss. Having an incident response plan ensures that when a cyber security incident occurs, a plan is in place to respond appropriately to the situation. In most situations, the aim of the response will be to prevent the cyber security incident from escalating, restore any impacted system or data, and preserve any evidence.[35]

Organisations should ask themselves several questions to determine how prepared they are to respond to cyber security incidents. These include identifying systems and data critical to business operations, having business continuity and disaster recovery plans, having an up-to-date and regularly tested cyber security incident response plan, including cyber security incident reporting and response activities in agreements with service providers, having the ability to detect when cyber security incidents may have occurred, and being aware of legislative obligations regarding reporting cyber security incidents.[36]

When asked "How would you rate the effectiveness of your organisation's cyber incident response plan?" 34% of respondents stated 'effective', whilst 21% stated 'moderately effective'. This doesn't bode well for organisations if only one-third think they have effective incident response plans.

Interestingly, yet equally disappointing, 9% or respondents stated their incident response plan was 'very ineffective'.

Cyber incident response typically involves a team of experts who work together to assess the situation, identify the cause of the incident, contain the damage, and implement remediation measures. The goal of cyber incident response is to minimise the damage caused by the incident, protect sensitive information, and prevent similar incidents from occurring in the future. Specifically, organisations should deliberate:

Impact Assessment

The first step in decision making is to conduct a thorough impact assessment of the incident to understand the scope, nature, and severity of the attack. This information is used to prioritise response actions and to allocate resources as appropriate. Impact assessment is a critical component of the decision-making process. Considerations include:

- Identify the scope of the attack, including what systems, data, and applications have been affected.

- Assess the severity of the impact, including the potential financial, operational, reputational, and legal consequences.

- Determine the priority of response, focusing first on the most critical systems and data.

- Consider the potential for data loss or theft, and to take steps to mitigate this risk, such as implementing data backups or encryption.

- Assess the impact on customers or stakeholders and communicate effectively with those affected.

- Consider regulatory requirements and assess these requirements and ensure compliance.

Business Continuity

Analyse the potential impact of the cyber-attack on business operations and take steps to minimise disruptions and ensure the continued delivery of essential services. This may involve implementing disaster recovery plans, redirecting resources, and communicating with stakeholders. Considerations include:

- Identify critical business functions that need to be restored as quickly as possible after an attack. These may include key applications, systems, and data.

- Prioritise restoration efforts based on the impact of the attack and the criticality of the business function.

- Implement backup and recovery measures, such as regular data backups, offsite data storage, and redundant systems.

- Develop a communication plan that outlines how employees, customers, and stakeholders will be informed about the impact of the attack and the steps being taken to restore critical business functions.

- Test business continuity plans by conducting regular drills and exercises to identify areas for improvement and refine the plan as necessary.

- Consider third-party service providers and assess their readiness to respond to a cyber-attack and ensure that their business continuity plans are aligned with your own.

Legal and Regulatory Compliance

Define the legal and regulatory requirements that apply to the organisation and take steps to comply with them. This may involve reporting the incident to relevant authorities, cooperating with investigations, and providing notification to affected individuals. Considerations include:

- Data Protection Laws, including complying with relevant data protection laws, such as GDPR or NDB.

- Notification requirements, such as the need to report certain types of cyber incidents to relevant authorities, such as data protection regulators, within a specific timeframe. Failure to do so can result in significant fines and other penalties.

- Ensuring the incident response plan includes procedures for notifying relevant authorities, such as law enforcement, and for documenting the incident in order to comply with regulatory requirements.

- Preservation of evidence to support any subsequent investigations or legal proceedings.

- Compliance with industry regulations, such as finance and healthcare, which might be subject to specific regulatory frameworks that require additional considerations when responding to cyber attacks.

- Contractual obligations they have with customers, vendors or partners, and ensure that they are complying with any relevant contractual obligations.

Reputation Management

Determine the potential impact of the cyber-attack on the organisation's reputation and take steps to mitigate it. This may involve communicating with stakeholders, providing transparent and accurate information, and taking responsibility for the incident. Considerations include:

- Transparency, including what happened, what data was affected, and what steps the company is taking to address the issue, can help to build trust with customers, stakeholders, and the wider community.

- Communication with a well-defined communication plan that includes both internal and external stakeholders. This plan should outline who is responsible for communication, what messages should be conveyed, and when and how communication should take place.

- Speed or lack thereof can be seen as an indication that the company does not take the incident seriously, which can damage its reputation.

- Prioritising the response efforts based on the severity of the incident, for example, if the incident involved sensitive customer data, the company should prioritise informing the affected customers and implementing measures to protect their data.

- Proactive measures, such as regularly testing and updating security systems. This can demonstrate to stakeholders that the company takes cyber security seriously and is committed to protecting their data.

- Reputation monitoring via social media, news outlets, and other channels for mentions of the company and the cyber-attack can help the company to identify potential reputational risks and respond accordingly.

Cost-Benefit Analysis

Evaluate the cost-benefit of different response options, balancing the costs of recovery against the potential risks and consequences of not taking action. Considerations include:

- The potential costs of responding to a cyber-attack, including incident response services, legal and regulatory compliance, public relations, and potential damages to affected parties.

- The potential cost of business interruption due to a cyber-attack. This can include lost revenue, productivity, and reputational damage.

- Reviewing insurance policies to determine whether there is coverage for cyber incidents. This can help to offset some of the costs associated with responding to a cyber-attack.

- The cost of implementing cyber security measures to prevent future attacks. This can include upgrading systems, investing in cyber security training for employees, and implementing new security protocols.

- The potential cost of not taking any action in response to a cyber-attack. This can include regulatory fines, legal liabilities, and reputational damage.

Risk Management

Investigate the risk management aspects of the incident, such as the likelihood of the attack happening again and the potential impact of the attack on the organisation and its stakeholders. Considerations include:

1. Conducting a risk assessment to identify potential vulnerabilities in their systems and processes. This can help them to prioritise response efforts and allocate resources effectively.

2. Having a well-defined incident response plan that outlines roles and responsibilities, procedures for detecting and reporting incidents, and a communication plan. This plan should be reviewed and updated regularly to ensure that it is effective.

3. Implementing mitigation measures to reduce the likelihood of a cyber-attack, such as regular software updates, employee training on cyber security best

practices, and implementing multi-factor authentication.

4. Having a business continuity plan in place to ensure that critical business operations can continue in the event of a cyber-attack. This can include backup and recovery procedures, alternative communication channels, and alternative work locations.

5. Considering the risks associated with third-party vendors and partners, and implement measures to mitigate these risks. This can include conducting due diligence on vendors and partners, implementing contractual requirements for cyber security, and regular monitoring of third-party systems.

Ethics and Values

Evaluate the ethical and value-based aspects of the incident, such as protecting the privacy of individuals and maintaining the trust of stakeholders. Considerations include:

- Being transparent about the incident and their response efforts. This can help to build trust with customers, stakeholders, and the wider community.

- Considering the privacy implications of their response efforts, particularly when dealing with sensitive data. This should ensure compliance with relevant privacy regulations and ethical standards.

- Ensuring response efforts do not discriminate against any individuals or groups. This includes ensuring all affected individuals receive equal treatment and that no one is unfairly targeted or excluded.

- Ensuring response efforts are fair and just, taking into account the needs and interests of all stakeholders.

- Taking responsibility for actions and impact on others. This includes acknowledging mistakes and taking steps to rectify them, as well as implementing measures to prevent similar incidents in the future.

- Showing respect for the dignity and rights of all individuals involved in the incident, including affected customers and employees, as well as the wider community.

External Experts

Deployment of external experts, such as incident response firms and legal counsel, to provide additional expertise and support during the incident response. Considerations include:

- The provision of specialised knowledge and expertise in responding to a cyber-attack, including in areas such as digital forensics, incident response, and legal and regulatory compliance.

- The need to respond quickly and efficiently to a cyber-attack, which can help to minimise the impact of the incident and reduce downtime.

- The need for an objective perspective on the incident, which can help to ensure the response is effective and appropriate.

- The need for a level of confidentiality and discretion that may be difficult for internal teams to achieve, particularly in cases where sensitive information is involved.

- The expense involved and if the potential costs against the potential benefits of using them.

- The requirement to work with reputable and trustworthy external experts, to avoid any potential conflicts of interest or other issues.

Ultimately, the decision-making process during a cyber-attack response requires a balance of technical knowledge, business acumen, and strategic thinking to respond to the incident while minimising the negative impact effectively and efficiently on the organisation and its stakeholders.

Research[37] aimed to identify the factors that influence individuals' behaviour in response to ransomware security incidents surveyed individuals who had experienced a ransomware security incident in the past and used logistic regression to analyse the data and identify the factors that influenced threat avoidance behaviour.

The study found that knowledge about ransomware is a significant predictor of threat avoidance behaviour. Individuals who had greater knowledge about ransomware were more likely to take steps to avoid threats, such as regularly backing up their data and updating their security software. This finding underscores the importance of education and training programs aimed at improving public knowledge about ransomware and how to protect against it.

The study also found the perceived severity of the threat and the perceived susceptibility to the threat were significant predictors of threat avoidance behaviour. Individuals who perceived ransomware to be a severe threat and believed that they were susceptible to it were more likely to take steps to avoid the threat. This highlights the importance of effective risk communication strategies that can accurately convey the severity and likelihood of harm from ransomware to the public.

Interestingly, the study found that trust in security software and the perceived effectiveness of security software were not significant predictors of threat avoidance behaviour. This suggests that individuals may not always rely solely on security software to protect themselves against ransomware threats and may also take other steps to protect their data.

The authors suggest their findings can be used to inform the development of effective strategies for mitigating the impact of ransomware incidents. This includes education and training programs aimed at improving public knowledge about ransomware, as well as risk communication strategies that accurately convey the severity and likelihood of harm from ransomware.

Additional research[38] into ransomware response proposes a decision framework for incident response teams to respond to ransomware attacks. The framework consists of six phases: preparation, detection, containment, eradication, recovery, and lessons learned. The study also highlights the importance of communication and collaboration during a ransomware attack. This may involve engaging external parties, such as law enforcement or cyber security experts, and ensuring that all stakeholders are kept informed throughout the incident response process.

Further research[39] into the incident response of a large healthcare provider that was targeted by a ransomware attack highlight several findings related to the detection and response to ransomware attacks:

1. Effective detection and response tools are critical: This is to quickly identify and respond to ransomware attacks. In this case, the healthcare provider was able to quickly detect and respond to the ransomware attack due to the use of security monitoring tools and a robust incident response plan.

2. Communication and coordination are key: This relates to stakeholder engagement during a ransomware attack, including IT, security, legal, and management. In this case, the healthcare provider was able to effectively coordinate the response to the ransomware attack due to the use of clear escalation paths and communication protocols.

3. Backup and recovery processes are critical: This is to ensure that critical data can be quickly restored in the event of a ransomware attack. In this case, the healthcare provider was able to quickly restore critical data from backups and minimise the impact of the ransomware attack.

4. Preparation is key: This includes regular training, testing, and updating of incident response plans. In this case, the healthcare provider was able to effectively respond to the ransomware attack due to the organisation's robust incident response plan and regular training and testing of response procedures.

Further research[40] into the development and implementation of a Cyber Security Incident Handling, Warning, and Response System (CyberSANE) tailored for safeguarding European Critical Information Infrastructures, highlights the integration of machine learning algorithms, threat intelligence feeds, and collaborative incident response features, positioning

CyberSANE as an innovative solution in the cyber security domain.

The research offers substantial technical contributions, including the CyberSANE architecture, threat modelling framework, and incident response workflow, which provide valuable insights for cyber security practitioners, system architects, and researchers working on incident handling and response systems. It adopts an interdisciplinary approach, blending principles from computer science, cyber security, and critical infrastructure protection. This perspective underscores the significance of collaboration between these domains to develop effective solutions for safeguarding critical infrastructures.

Another model is the CREST maturity model to enable assessment of the status of an organisation's cyber security incident response capability. The model has been supplemented by a spreadsheet-based maturity assessment tool which helps to measure the maturity of a cyber security incident response capability on a scale of 1 (least effective) to 5 (most effective). The tool is powerful yet easy to use and consists of two different spreadsheets, enabling assessments to be made at either a summary or detailed level.[41]

Research[42] addresses the critical challenges posed by modern cyber threats and offers a comprehensive exploration of the techniques and procedures necessary to respond effectively to such threats recognising the evolving nature of cyber threats and the need to equip cyber security professionals with the knowledge and tools required to combat these threats effectively. It highlights the need for a systematic approach to handling cyber incidents, from initial detection to post-incident analysis. It also takes an interdisciplinary approach by connecting the dots between digital forensics, incident response, and cyber security. It recognises that these domains are intrinsically linked and must work together seamlessly to effectively respond to cyber threats.

With the constant threat of cybercrime, cyber security professionals must be on high alert for potential attacks and cyber security incidents, as they can negatively impact the organisation they work for. Unfortunately, cyber attacks can occur outside the 9-5 workday, meaning there's a constant threat team members may worry about. Excessively worrying about work-related issues can contribute heavily to employees' feelings and symptoms of burnout. Burnout is a state of emotional, physical, and mental exhaustion caused by prolonged exposure to stress. A study has found 65% of respondents considered leaving their jobs due to stress and 73% of respondents had to resign due to burnout.[43]

Another reason for burnout is the unrealistic expectations to meet. In addition to constant cyber threats, the expectations and responsibilities of cyber security professionals can quickly become overwhelming. The field is complex and can be incredibly intimidating for people new to the industry. Employees may feel they need more motivation to meet their roles' expectations, particularly if they're not receiving any recognition or appreciation from management or the C-suite.

Isolation in roles as another factor contributing to cyber security burnout. In the remote work era, isolation is an issue for millions of people. If cyber security professionals work remotely, they have little opportunity to socialise with co-workers, especially those working in other departments of their organisation. People who collaborate with their co-workers tend to feel more satisfied with their work, often reach higher levels of productivity and are less likely to experience symptoms of burnout.[44]

When asked "How often do you experience feelings of burnout after responding to a cyber security incident?" 42% stated 'most of the time', whilst another 31% said 'sometimes'. When asked "When faced with a particularly challenging cyber security incident, how do you typically cope with the stress?" the highest two responses were 'Engaging in problem-solving activities to address the issues that led to the incident' and 'Distracting yourself with hobbies or activities unrelated to the incident'. Comments provided included playing golf, going to the pub with mates, eating chocolate, drinking alcohol, and going for a walk.

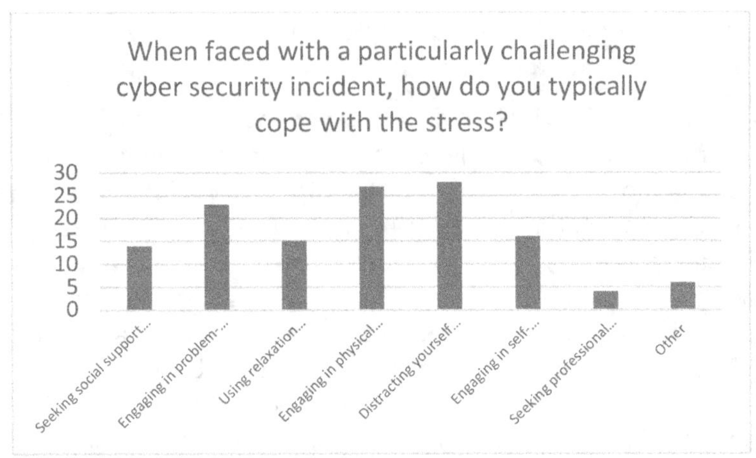

Making Decisions

Decision making is the process of selecting a course of action or choosing from among several alternatives to achieve a desired goal or solve a problem. It involves evaluating available options, considering their potential outcomes and consequences, and then making a choice. Decision making can be rational, following a systematic and logical approach, or it can be intuitive, relying on instinct and gut feelings. It is a fundamental aspect of human cognition and is crucial in various aspects of life, including business, education, personal relationships, and problem-solving situations.

Effective decision making involves critical thinking, analysis, and often, a balance between logic and intuition. During a crisis, decision-making processes often become more challenging and complex due to the heightened stress, time pressure, and uncertainty inherent in crisis situations.

Decision making during any crisis, including the response to a cyber attack, is a complex process that involves several different factors. Some of the key aspects of decision making during a crisis include:

1. Time pressure: Crises often involve a high degree of time pressure, which can make decision making more difficult. Decision makers must be able to quickly assess the situation and make decisions in a timely manner to mitigate the impact of the crisis.

2. Information gathering: To make informed decisions during a crisis, decision makers must gather as much information as possible about the situation. This may involve collecting data from a variety of sources, such as first responders, witnesses, and experts.

3. Risk assessment: Decision makers must be able to assess the potential risks and consequences of their decisions. This may involve evaluating the likelihood of different outcomes and determining the potential impact of different courses of action.

4. Communication: Effective communication is crucial during a crisis. Decision makers must be able to communicate their decisions clearly and effectively to those who will be affected by them. This may include communicating with the public, first responders, and other stakeholders.

5. Collaboration: Decision making during a crisis often involves multiple stakeholders, including government agencies, private organisations, and community groups. Decision makers must be able to collaborate effectively with these stakeholders to make informed decisions.

6. Adaptability: Crises are often unpredictable, and decision makers must be able to adapt to changing circumstances. This may involve revising decisions as new information becomes available, or adjusting plans as the situation evolves.

7. Resilience: Decision making during a crisis can be emotionally and physically demanding. Decision makers must be able to maintain their focus and resilience to make effective decisions, even in the face of adversity.

8. Ethical considerations: Decision making during a crisis can raise complex ethical questions. Decision makers must be aware of the potential ethical implications of their decisions and strive to make choices that are consistent with the values of the organisation and society.

When the survey respondents were asked "How satisfied are you with the communication and coordination among team members during the incident response process?", 43% said they were 'moderately satisfied', followed by 25% who were 'neither satisfied or unsatisfied. When asked "When responding to a cyber security incident, do you feel that your organisation provides you with sufficient resources and tools?", pleasingly, 53% stated 'yes'.

How satisfied are you with the communication
and coordination among team members during
the incident response process?
30
25
20
15
10
5
0
Extremely
dissatisfied
Somewhat
dissatisfied
Neither
satisfied nor
dissatisfied
Moderately
satisfied
Extremely
satisfied

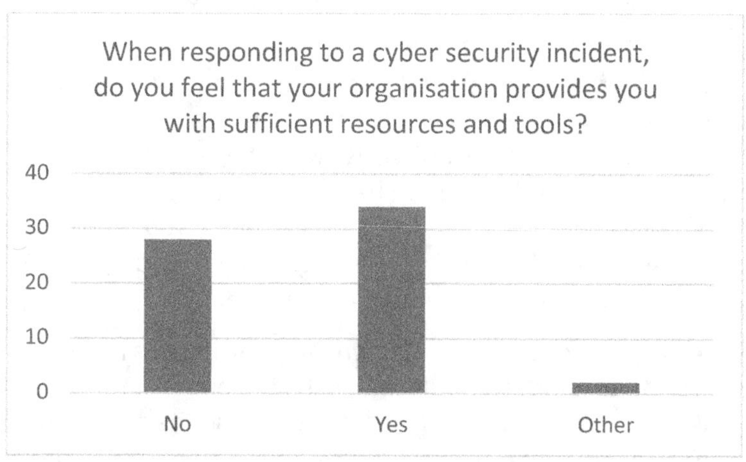
When responding to a cyber security incident,
do you feel that your organisation provides you
with sufficient resources and tools?
40
30
20
10
0
No
Yes
Other

In the realm of cyber security, individuals and organisations often face hidden or latent vulnerabilities and threats that may not be immediately apparent. These hidden risks can be likened to the concept of unconscious conflicts. Just as Freud's theory suggests that unresolved conflicts can impact behaviour, undetected security vulnerabilities can lead to cyber incidents if not identified and addressed.[45]

Sigmund Freud's theory of psychoanalysis is a personality theory that focuses on unconscious mental processes and their influence on human behaviour. According to Freud, the psyche comprises three aspects: the id, ego, and superego. The id is entirely unconscious (being the primitive and instinctual part of the mind), while the ego operates in the conscious mind. The superego operates both unconsciously and consciously.[46]

Freud's theory of the mental apparatus suggests that human behaviour is influenced by unconscious memories, thoughts, and urges. In the context of decision-making during a crisis, Freud's theory of the ego can be applied. The ego is responsible for mediating between the unrealistic id and the real external world. Ideally, the ego works by reason, whereas the id is chaotic and unreasonable.[47]

In a crisis, the ego may be overwhelmed by the id's irrational demands, leading to impulsive and irrational decision-making. Therefore, it is essential to recognise the role of the ego in decision-making during a crisis and to work towards strengthening it.

Freud's theory of psychoanalysis suggests that human behaviour is influenced by unconscious mental processes, and the ego plays a crucial role in mediating between the id and the external world. In a crisis, the ego may be overwhelmed by the id's irrational demands, leading to impulsive and irrational decision-making. Therefore, it is essential to recognise the role of the ego in decision-making during a crisis and to work towards strengthening it.

A study[48] of CSIRTs from government, academia, and private sector teams provided insights across multiple aspects of incident response, including information sharing, organisation, learning, and automation. The research highlights the importance of contextual awareness in informing design and engineering, as well as the need to focus on vertical integration of issues at different levels of the incident response system. The study also provides insights into the challenges faced by network defenders in cyber security incident response, including time pressures. The authors suggest that the lack of broad contextual understanding may be biasing approaches to improving operations and driving faulty assumptions in cyber teams.

Constant decision making is a hallmark in cyber security, including:

- The continuous monitoring of networks, systems, and endpoints for signs of malicious activity.

- In the event of a cyber incident, decisions are made around predefined response actions, such as isolating affected systems.

- Visual representations of cyber security data, such as dashboards and heat maps.

- The use of threat intelligence feeds, enabling organisations to stay updated on the latest cyber threats and vulnerabilities.

- Assessing risk associated with various cyber security decisions.

In the context of decision-making during a cyber security incident, it is essential to recognise the role of the ego in decision-making and to work towards strengthening it. Many cyber incidents are human-enabled, and it is more vital to focus on social and behavioural issues to improve the current situation. Research[49] suggests decision-making frameworks such as multi-criteria decision-making (MCDM) can be used to back a decision. MCDA provides a means of structuring complex decision-making processes conducted with multiple stakeholders.

In the context of cyber incident response, MCDM can be used to prioritise all-hazard threats and develop containment, eradication, and recovery strategies based on criteria such as the criticality of the affected assets, the type and severity of the incident, the need to preserve evidence, the importance of any affected systems to critical business processes, and the resources required to implement the strategy.[50]

Other research[51] into decision-making during a cyber security incident, suggests two types of decision-making are required: event-based decision-making and risk-based decision-making. Event-based decision-making is faster, tactical, and necessary for day-to-day choices, while risk-based decision-making is required for strategic investments.

Decision support systems play a pivotal role in cyber security for several compelling reasons. Firstly, the cyber threat landscape is dynamic, characterised by a constant influx of new threats and vulnerabilities. Cyber adversaries continually adapt and evolve their tactics. In such an environment, human decision-makers need timely and accurate information to make informed choices in response to emerging threats.

Secondly, cyber security incidents can have severe consequences. From data breaches to ransomware attacks, the impact can extend to financial losses, reputational damage, and even compromise of national security. Therefore, swift and effective decision-making is essential to mitigate these risks.

Thirdly, the volume and complexity of data in cyber security operations are staggering. Security logs, threat intelligence feeds, network traffic data, and system alerts inundate security professionals daily. Decision support systems help distil this vast amount of information into actionable insights, enabling cyber security analysts to focus on the most critical threats.

Whilst there are undeniable benefits, implementing decision support systems in cyber security is not without challenges, including:

- The sheer volume of data generated by cyber security tools can overwhelm decision-makers.

- Integrating tools into a cohesive decision making ecosystem can be complex and require customisation.

- A high number of false positives can lead to alert fatigue among cyber security analysts.

A study[52] into the psychology of cyber security incident response, highlights several issues:

1. The importance of situational awareness: This refers to the ability to understand and analyse the situation at hand. Situational awareness is critical for effective incident response as it allows responders to make informed decisions and take appropriate actions.

2. The impact of cognitive biases: This can lead to errors in decision-making and actions. Cognitive biases can be particularly challenging in incident response as responders may be under significant stress and pressure to act quickly.

3. The role of emotions: This includes emotions such as fear, anger, and anxiety which can be particularly challenging in incident response as they can lead to irrational decision-making and behaviour.

4. The importance of communication: This is critical for coordination and collaboration between responders. Effective communication can also help to manage emotions and reduce cognitive biases.

5. The impact of organisational culture: This includes leadership, training, and resources. Organisational culture can influence the effectiveness of incident response by shaping the attitudes, behaviours, and skills of responders.

The healthcare sector, is an increasingly digitised landscape, where institutions are progressively relying on electronic health records, connected medical devices, and telehealth systems. However, this digital transformation has also exposed healthcare providers to cyber security vulnerabilities. Research[53] related to cyber incident response centres on exploring the strategies, tools, and frameworks for Effective, Analytical, and Resilient Security (EARS) to counteract cyber incidents specifically within healthcare settings.

EARS is designed to address the unique cyber security challenges faced by healthcare organisations. It emphasises the need for security measures to be not only effective but also analytical and resilient. The framework provides a structured approach for healthcare institutions to enhance their cyber security posture by enabling them to proactively detect, respond to, and recover from cyber incidents.

The research takes an interdisciplinary approach, recognising that cyber security in healthcare necessitates collaboration among healthcare professionals, IT experts, and policymakers. It highlights the importance of fostering a culture of cyber security within healthcare organisations and engaging various stakeholders in developing a unified cyber security strategy.

Further research[54] on cyber security incident handling within critical infrastructure is the Introduction and exploration of a modelling language framework. This framework offers a structured approach to incident response by enabling the modelling and representation of various aspects of the incident handling process. It provides incident responders with a comprehensive toolkit for identifying, assessing, mitigating, and recovering from cyber security incidents effectively.

It delves into the intricate and evolving cyber threat landscape that confronts the critical infrastructure sector. It underscores the vulnerabilities of these infrastructures, emphasising the potential consequences of cyber attacks on essential services, public safety, and national security.

It also advocates for interdisciplinary collaboration in the field of cyber security incident handling for critical infrastructures. It recognises that incident response involves not only technical aspects but also legal, regulatory, and organisational considerations. This holistic approach ensures that incident responders are well-equipped to navigate the complex landscape of critical infrastructure cyber security.

Human capacity limitations in the context of cognitive processing of data make incident response a challenging task. Managers often need to make quick decisions and take mitigating measures based on their awareness of the situation at that moment, which is often limited and sometimes biased. Support that could help alleviate some of these challenges and assist in defensive cyber operations is highly desirable.[55]

Research[56] into how incident response teams are faced with an increasingly demanding environment and as a result face many cognitive challenges. Although some forms of decision support have been developed, these tend to be linear and procedural, have the potential to consume too many mental resources, and are frequently not geared to unexpected and difficult cyberattacks, all of which undermines compliance and effectiveness. Moreover, these forms of decision support have mostly not been informed by the results of an analysis of the cognitive demands and requirements faced by defensive cyber responders. The following observations were made:

1. Relevant expertise and knowledge appears to be mostly acquired throughout an individual's career path, over the years, but not through education.

2. Communication with external parties such as threat intelligence networks, outsourced service providers and third parties; with internal stakeholders ranging from technical people to business and strategic actors within the organisation; and team members to get or deliver information, be it a request for specific actions, information or actionable intelligence is difficult.

3. Environmental conditions and external stimuli influence the quality of the work of incident responders. This includes time pressure, other people (consciously or not), or by the organisation.

4. Time pressure on incident responders acts as blinders, and may prevent them from maintaining an overview of the bigger picture.

Research[57] into cyber security threat and incident management, aiming to enhance decision support for cyber security professionals found organisations face relentless cyber security challenges, necessitating sophisticated decision support systems. The research emphasised the importance of developing decision support tools tailored to the specific needs of cyber security threat and incident managers. This is due to the complexity and velocity of cyber threats, which demand rapid and informed decisions. The authors argue that decision support tools are essential for threat and incident managers to navigate this intricate landscape effectively. Such decision making tools need to include threat intelligence integration, incident response orchestration, and data visualisation.

Additionally, a human-centric approach to decision support is required because cyber security is not solely a technical challenge but also a cognitive one, involving human decision-makers. The research delves into cognitive processes, decision-making biases, and human-computer interaction to design decision support systems that align seamlessly with the cognitive demands of cyber security professionals.[58]

Further, there is a need for collaboration between cyber security experts, cognitive psychologists, and human-computer interaction specialists. This collaboration ensures that decision support tools are not only technically sound but also cognitively aligned with the needs of human decision-makers. As the cyber security landscape continues to evolve, decision support systems of this nature become increasingly indispensable in bolstering cyber resilience and safeguarding organisations against emerging threats.[59]

Howard Gardner's Theory of Multiple Intelligences[60] suggests that there are multiple forms of intelligence, and individuals may excel in different areas. While Gardner's theory is typically applied to educational contexts, its concepts can be adapted to inform the development of more user-friendly and effective cyber incident response tools and systems:

1. Linguistic Intelligence: This type of intelligence relates to language skills. In the context of cyber incident response, linguistic intelligence can be leveraged to develop clear and concise communication channels and documentation. Incident response tools and platforms can prioritise plain language explanations, making them more accessible to a wider range of users.

2. Logical-Mathematical Intelligence: Logical-mathematical intelligence involves problem-solving and analytical thinking. Incident response tools can incorporate logical and mathematical models to help analysts and responders identify patterns, analyse data, and make informed decisions more efficiently. These tools can also provide interactive simulations for incident scenario analysis.

3. Spatial Intelligence: Spatial intelligence involves an individual's ability to visualise and work with spatial information. In incident response, spatial intelligence can be applied to create intuitive and visually engaging interfaces for incident dashboards and data visualisation tools. Such tools can help responders better understand the scope and impact of an incident.

4. Interpersonal Intelligence: Interpersonal intelligence pertains to understanding and interacting effectively with others. In the context of incident response, tools and systems can include collaboration features that facilitate communication and coordination among response teams. Virtual war rooms and chat platforms can encourage teamwork during cyber incidents.

5. Intrapersonal Intelligence: Intrapersonal intelligence relates to self-awareness and self-regulation. Incident response tools can incorporate features that help individuals manage stress and make informed decisions during high-pressure situations. This might include guidance on self-care and stress management techniques.

6. Musical and Kinaesthetic Intelligence: While less directly applicable to incident response, these intelligences can inform creative elements of user interface design. Elements like sound cues and user-friendly touch or gesture controls can enhance the usability and engagement of incident response tools.

7. Naturalistic Intelligence: Naturalistic intelligence involves an appreciation for the natural world. While this may not have a direct application in incident response tools, it does emphasise the importance of considering the user's environment and context when designing these tools. For example, incident response apps should be adaptable for use in different work settings and situations.

When asked "How concerned are you about the potential negative consequences of responding to cyber security incidents on your personal life or well-being?", 42% of respondents stated "neither positive or negative', followed by 34% of respondents stating 'somewhat negative'.

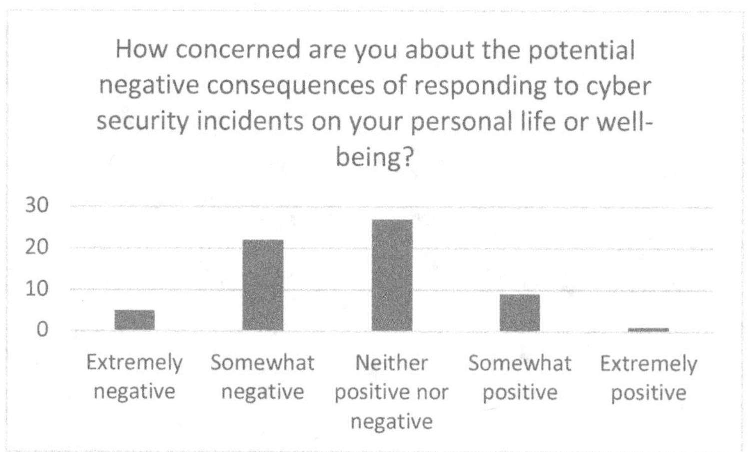

When asked "Which emotions do you typically experience during a cyber security incident response?" the two highest responses were 'frustration' at 21% and 'Determination' at 20%, followed by 'anxiety' at 17%. Survey participants were allowed to select all emotions which they felt, with a broad cross-section of responses.

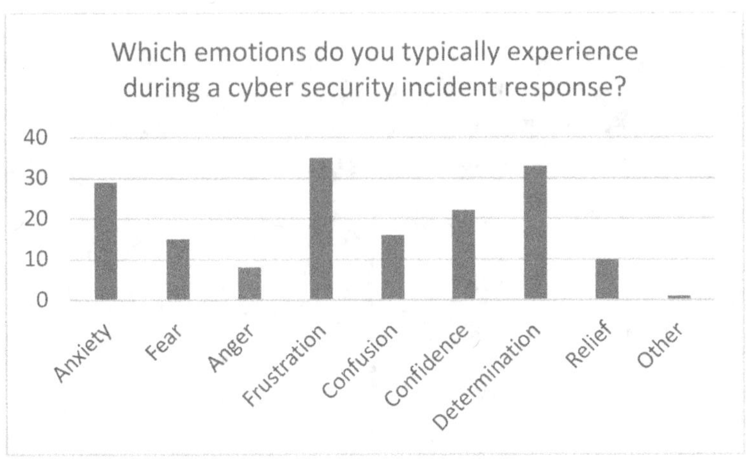

Incident responders during a cyber attack often experience a range of emotions due to the high-stress nature of their work. The initial realisation of the attack may lead to a state of shock. This shock can sometimes be followed by a phase of denial, where the gravity of the situation is hard to accept.[61]

As the reality of the situation sets in, responders may feel guilt, especially if they believe they could have done something to prevent the attack. This guilt can be accompanied by anger due to frustration with the situation.

The urgency and potential damage of the situation can lead to feelings of panic and fear. Anxiety is also common, given the pressure to resolve the issue and mitigate damage. The overall situation can be highly stressful, with two-thirds of cyber security incident responders reporting stress or anxiety in their daily lives due to their profession.[62]

These emotions can significantly impact the effectiveness and speed of recovery, including key decisions about how to respond to the attack. Therefore, it's important for response teams to anticipate and proactively address the emotional impact of these high-stress attacks. This can include measures to control emotions, protect team members' well-being, and ensure better decision-making during a cyberattack.

When asked "How would you describe your ability to maintain focus and concentration during a cyber security incident response?", 53% of respondents stated 'good', followed by 30% stating 'excellent'.

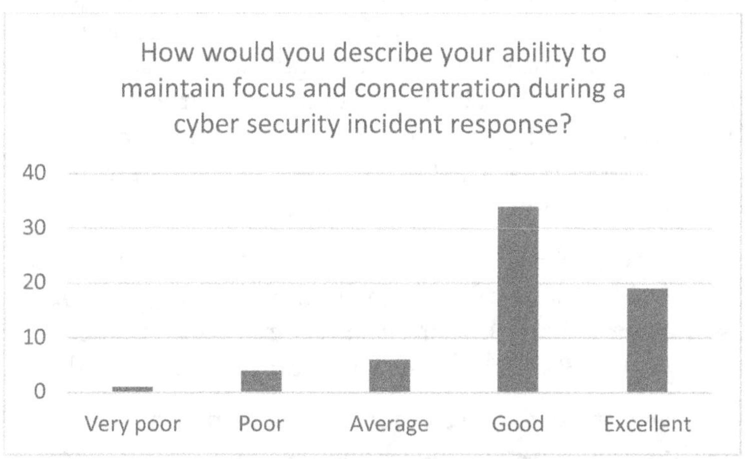

Keeping focus and concentration during a cyber attack is crucial for an incident responder. One of the key attributes that can help is having up-to-date knowledge of IT security hardware, software, and solutions. This knowledge forms the foundation for understanding the nature of the threat and how to counter it.

Another important attribute is proficiency in programming and scripting languages, understanding the typologies of attacks and attacker techniques which can be beneficial in understanding the attack and formulating a response.

A problem-solving mindset is another critical attribute. This mindset can help in identifying and mitigating threats effectively. Cyber security is a team effort, and the ability to work well in a team is crucial. The ability to react quickly and efficiently under pressure is vital during a cyber attack.

Emotional resilience is another key attribute. Maintaining composure in high-stress situations can help in making clear decisions. Finally, taking care of one's mental and physical health can enhance focus and concentration. These attributes can significantly improve an incident responder's effectiveness during a cyber attack. It's important to note that these attributes can be developed and strengthened over time with practice and experience.

When asked "How confident are you in your ability to effectively manage stress arising from responding to a cyber security incident?", 33% or respondents stated 'confident', followed by 25% stating they were 'somewhat confident'.

Managing stress during a cyber incident response is crucial for the effectiveness of the response and the health of the team. High-stress situations can significantly impact the effectiveness and speed of recovery, including key decisions about how to restore systems. Allowing incident responders time away to rest and heal from the heightened stress of cyber incidents will help keep teams healthy and prepared for the next attack. Prolonged high-stress situations can have negative effects on the team's health. Managing stress is important for workload management, mitigating the emotional impact on the team members, enhancing team performance, and optimal allocation of resources.

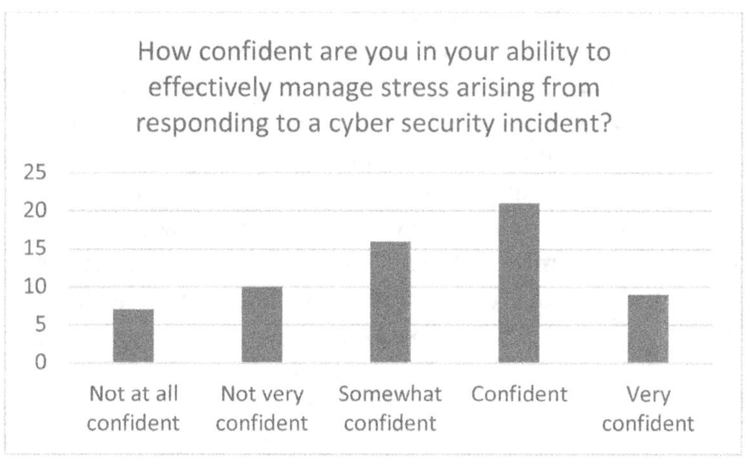

Leading on from this, when asked "Have you ever sought professional help or counselling to cope with stressful effects of cyber security incident response?", 70% stated 'no'.

Seeking professional help or counselling is vital in managing the stressful effects of cyber security incident response. High-stress situations can significantly impact the effectiveness and speed of recovery, including key decisions about how to restore systems. Professional help can provide strategies and techniques to manage and contain this stress, enhancing team performance and cohesion. It can also equip the cyber incident response team to cope with challenging circumstances through incident simulations that stress-test difficult decision scenarios. Moreover, professional help can improve employee well-being, more effective collaboration, and better performance.[63]

In addition, professional help can assist in recognising signs of anxiety and stress, so they can be better managed, individually and as part of a team. A recent study[64] concluded nearly two-thirds of incident responders have sought mental health assistance (almost the reverse of my survey findings) as a result of responding to cybersecurity incidents. Allowing incident responders time away to rest and heal from the heightened stress of cyber incidents will help keep teams healthy and prepared for the next attack. Furthermore, professional help can provide support to assist the recovery of normal individuals experiencing normal distress following exposure to abnormal events.

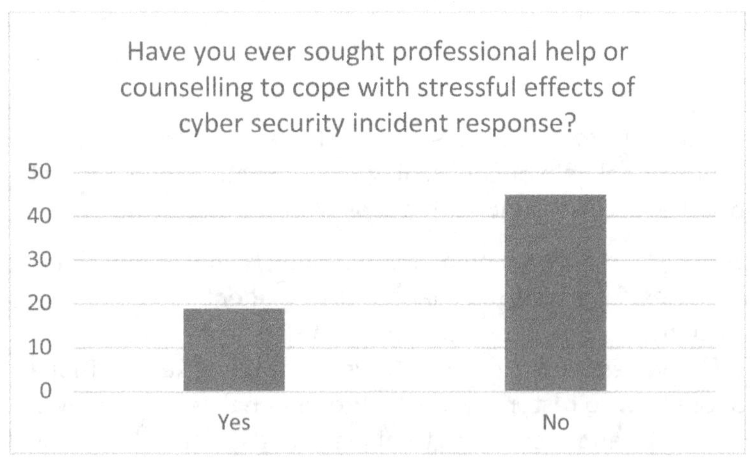

Human Factors

Human factors in cyber security refer to the psychological, social, and behavioural aspects of human beings that can affect the security of computer systems and networks. These factors include human errors, such as poor password management, and falling for phishing attacks, as well as deliberate actions, such as insider threats and social engineering attacks. Human factors can also include the impact of stress, workload, and fatigue on security decision-making, as well as organisational culture and leadership. Understanding human factors in cyber security and indeed response to cybercrime attacks is critical to developing effective security strategies that consider the role of humans in the security ecosystem.

While the technical aspects of cyber security, such as firewalls, encryption, and intrusion detection systems, are undoubtedly vital, it is imperative to recognise that cyber security is not solely a technical challenge. Instead, it is a multifaceted domain that hinges on human decision-makers navigating the complex landscape of cyber threats.

To comprehend the cognitive dimension of cyber security, it is important to consider the evolution of cyber threats. In the early days of the internet, cyber security primarily revolved around technical fortifications against viruses and malware. However, today's threat landscape is characterised by sophisticated adversaries who employ social engineering, phishing, and psychological manipulation to breach systems and networks. These threats exploit the cognitive vulnerabilities of humans rather than solely targeting technical weaknesses. As a result, cyber security has transcended its purely technical origins to incorporate the intricacies of human cognition.

An important aspect when considering human factors is the celebration and ongoing training and support of internet users as the strongest detection point in the defence chain. It is important we change the narrative from that of end-users being the weakest link, to that celebrating the role of individuals to identify and report a potential cyber incident. This will only occur through concerted communications and adjustments to organisational culture.

Despite the presence of robust technical defences, cyber criminals recognise that human decision-makers are susceptible to manipulation and deception. Phishing attacks, for instance, leverage psychological tactics to trick individuals into divulging sensitive information or clicking on malicious links. This underscores the cognitive aspect of cyber security, where human judgment, decision-making, and behaviour become critical determinants of cyber resilience.

Human decision-makers are not immune to cognitive biases, which can significantly impact cyber security. Confirmation bias, overconfidence, and anchoring are just a few examples of cognitive biases that can lead to suboptimal security decisions. For example, confirmation bias might cause an individual to dismiss warning signs of a cyber threat because they align with preconceived notions. Recognising and mitigating these biases is a vital aspect of enhancing cyber security posture.[65]

In response to the cognitive challenges posed by cyber threats, the concept of cognitive resilience has emerged. Cognitive resilience refers to the ability of individuals and organisations to withstand and recover from cognitive attacks, such as social engineering or manipulation. It involves education and training to enhance cyber security awareness, improve decision-making skills, and foster a culture of vigilance. The goal is to fortify the human element of cyber security alongside technical defences.[66]

Effective cyber security necessitates the intersection between human and technical elements. Technical defences alone cannot guarantee protection against threats that exploit human cognitive vulnerabilities. Conversely, human decision-makers, no matter how informed, may struggle to navigate the intricacies of cyber threats without the support of robust technical systems. The intersection of technical and human elements in cyber security incident response is a critical aspect of effective incident management. Technical elements refer to the use of technology and tools to detect, prevent, and respond to cyber threats. Human elements, on the other hand, refer to the people involved in the incident response process, including decision-makers, responders, and stakeholders.

Effective incident response requires a balance between technical and human elements. Technical elements can help automate and streamline the incident response process, including triage, containment, analysis, remediation, and recovery, but they cannot replace human decision-making and judgment. Human elements are essential for interpreting and contextualizing technical data, making decisions, and communicating with stakeholders and are just as important as technology to a successful response.[67]

There has been significant academic research into this area, with each study building on previous work and corroborating consistent themes when analysing decision making processes during a cyber incident response.

A study[68] into the role of human factors in cyber security incident response identified several key human factors that can impact incident response. The authors emphasised the importance of cognitive factors, such as perception, attention, and memory, in incident response. They noted that cognitive biases, such as confirmation bias and anchoring bias, can impact decision-making and increase the risk of errors. To mitigate these biases, the authors recommend using structured decision-making processes and providing training on cognitive biases.

The authors highlighted the importance of social factors, such as communication and teamwork, in incident response. Effective communication is critical for sharing information and coordinating actions among responders. The authors recommend using clear and concise language, establishing communication protocols, and conducting regular training on communication skills. Teamwork is also important for incident response, and the authors recommend developing a shared mental model among responders and establishing clear roles and responsibilities.

The authors also discuss the impact of organisational factors, such as leadership, culture, and resources, on incident response. Effective leadership is critical for setting the tone and priorities for incident response. Establishing a strong incident response team with clear roles and responsibilities, providing sufficient resources for incident response, and conducting regular training and exercises to build skills and maintain readiness. Organisational culture is also important, as it can influence the attitudes and behaviours of responders. A culture of open communication, accountability, and continuous improvement is required.

A study[69] into the psychological factors that can influence the effectiveness of cyber security incident response identified several key findings. The authors emphasised the importance of managing emotions during incident response. They noted that incidents can be stressful and emotionally challenging, which can impact decision-making and increase the risk of errors. Effective incident response requires responders to remain calm and focused, and to avoid becoming overwhelmed by their emotions. Organisations should provide training on stress management and emotional regulation, and creating a supportive environment that encourages self-care and well-being.

The authors highlight the importance of cognitive factors, such as attention, memory, and decision-making, in incident response. They note that incidents can be complex and require rapid decision-making, which can be challenging under stressful conditions. Effective incident response requires responders to have strong cognitive skills, including the ability to process information quickly and accurately, and to make decisions based on limited information. To support this, the authors recommend providing training on cognitive skills, such as attention and memory, and creating a decision-making framework that enables responders to make informed decisions quickly.

The authors discuss the importance of collaboration in incident response. They note that incidents often require the participation of multiple individuals and teams, and that effective collaboration is essential for sharing information and coordinating actions. To support collaboration, organisations need to create a collaborative culture that encourages open communication and mutual respect, and providing training on collaboration skills, such as effective communication and conflict resolution.

The study explores the role of psychological factors in cyber security incident response and identifies several key factors that impact the effectiveness of incident response. The authors emphasise that effective incident response is not only dependent on technical expertise but also on the psychological factors that influence the actions and decision-making of incident responders.

Another study[70] which follows these themes highlights a range of psychological factors as important for effective incident response. Firstly, the authors note the way incident responders perceive risk can significantly impact their actions during incident response. Responders who perceive the incident as high-risk are more likely to take appropriate actions and respond quickly. On the other hand, responders who perceive the incident as low-risk may not take the incident seriously, leading to a delayed or inadequate response. To improve incident response, the authors recommend increasing awareness of the potential risks and consequences of cyber incidents.

The authors also highlighted that cognitive biases can impact decision-making during incident response. Responders may have biases towards certain solutions or courses of action, leading to suboptimal decision-making. To address this organisations should create decision-making frameworks that encourage objective and rational decision-making.

Additionally the authors noted incident response can be a highly stressful and emotionally taxing task, which can impact the decision-making and actions of responders. Responders who are experiencing stress or negative emotions may be more likely to make mistakes or take suboptimal actions. Finally, the authors emphasised the importance of effective communication and teamwork during incident response. Poor communication and teamwork can lead to misunderstandings, delays, and suboptimal decision-making. The provision of training on effective communication and teamwork skills, as well as creating communication protocols and processes that facilitate collaboration and information sharing.

Another study[71] proposes a human factors framework for cyber incident response, which takes into account the psychological and social factors that influence the effectiveness of incident response. The authors identified several key factors that are important for incident response success. They include the importance of maintaining situational awareness during incident response. This involves understanding the current state of the incident and being able to anticipate future developments. Effective incident response requires responders to have a clear understanding of the situation and the context in which it is occurring.

The authors also highlighted the importance of decision-making during incident response. They noted effective decision-making requires responders to be able to weigh the available options and make informed choices based on the best available information. Further the authors highlighted the importance of communication during incident response. They noted effective communication is essential for coordinating actions and sharing information between different teams and individuals.

Finally, the authors emphasised the importance of teamwork in incident response. They noted that incidents often require the participation of multiple individuals and teams, and that effective teamwork is essential for sharing information and coordinating actions. Creating a collaborative culture that encourages open communication and mutual respect, and providing training on teamwork skills, such as effective communication and conflict resolution.

Corroborating these findings, additional academic research explores the role of the human factor in cyber security incident response and highlights the importance of understanding human behaviour and cognition in effective incident response. The study[72] highlights cognitive biases can significantly impact the decision-making of incident responders. Responders may have biases towards certain solutions or courses of action, leading to suboptimal decision-making. Further, the authors emphasise the importance of effective communication and collaboration in incident response. Poor communication and collaboration can lead to misunderstandings, delays, and suboptimal decision-making.

Additionally the authors highlight the impact of stress and well-being on incident response. Incident response can be a highly stressful and emotionally taxing task, which can impact the decision-making and actions of responders. Finally, the authors note that experience and training can significantly impact the effectiveness of incident response. Responders with more experience and training are more likely to make effective decisions and take appropriate actions during incident response.

Another aspect of incident response is evolutionary psychology, grounded in the principles of evolutionary biology, examines how certain human behaviours and psychological traits have evolved over time to enhance survival and reproduction.[73] While this theory may not be directly applicable to the development of cyber threat intelligence, it can inform the understanding of human behaviours and decision-making in the context of cyber security:

1. Understanding Human Vulnerabilities: Evolutionary Psychology helps cyber security professionals recognise that certain human vulnerabilities, such as susceptibility to social engineering attacks, may be rooted in evolutionary adaptations. This understanding can guide the development of threat intelligence by focusing on the psychological aspects of cyber threats.

2. Risk Perception: Evolutionary Psychology sheds light on how humans perceive and respond to risks. For instance, individuals may prioritise immediate gains over long-term security, a bias that cybercriminals exploit. Threat intelligence can take these biases into account to predict and mitigate cyber risks effectively.

3. Trust and Suspicion: Evolutionary principles highlight the importance of trust and cooperation in human evolution. Cyber threat intelligence can benefit from insights into how humans establish trust online and what triggers suspicion. This knowledge can inform strategies to identify malicious actors and protect against cyber threats.

4. Behavioural Patterns: Evolutionary Psychology suggests that humans have evolved certain behavioural patterns, such as forming social groups for protection. These patterns can be applied to understand how cyber threat actors operate in

groups or networks and how threat intelligence can identify and disrupt these activities.

5. Deception and Detection: Understanding how humans have evolved to detect deception and signals of trustworthiness can inform the development of threat intelligence tools. By studying the cognitive processes involved in identifying online deception, cyber security professionals can create more effective detection mechanisms.

6. Human Error: Evolutionary Psychology acknowledges that humans are prone to cognitive biases and errors. In the context of cyber security, understanding these biases can help design threat intelligence systems that minimise the impact of human errors and improve incident response.

7. Adaptive Responses: Humans have evolved to adapt to changing environments. Similarly, threat intelligence must adapt to evolving cyber threats. By recognising the dynamic nature of cyber risks and attackers' strategies, threat intelligence can develop proactive measures to anticipate and counter emerging threats.

Considerations in Incident Response

Cyber threats are seldom one-dimensional being multifaceted, spanning technical, psychological, and strategic dimensions. They manifest as a blend of technical vulnerabilities, human error, and strategic manoeuvring. As cyber adversaries continuously refine their tactics, the traditional approach of solely relying on technical defences becomes insufficient. Decision-makers need a broader perspective that incorporates insights from various disciplines to understand, predict, and respond effectively to these evolving threats.

While technical expertise is foundational to cyber security, it is not the sole requirement for effective decision support. Interdisciplinary teams recognise that cyber security is more than just configuring firewalls or deploying antivirus software. It involves understanding the human element, including the psychology of cybercriminals and the biases affecting defenders' decisions. Additionally, it encompasses strategic aspects such as threat intelligence, incident response orchestration, and risk management.

The role of psychology is paramount in understanding both the adversaries' and defenders' behaviours. Cyber threat actors employ psychological tactics to manipulate and deceive individuals, making social engineering attacks a prevalent threat. Decision support systems must integrate insights from cognitive psychology to educate users about potential pitfalls and biases, ultimately bolstering cyber resilience. The role of psychology in understanding the adversaries' behaviours in a cyber response is to identify the motivations and methods of the attackers.

Behavioural analysis in security is a methodology for threat detection that focuses on understanding the behaviours of users and entities (servers, file shares, etc.) within your environment as well as the behaviours of adversaries, including their motivations and methods. By understanding the psychological levers that are pulled to trick victims, we can better prepare for cyber security threats and mitigate the risks associated with them. The progression of a cyber intrusion is determined by the attackers' future moves, their objectives, and their motivation, which characterises the malefactor's behaviour in the system.[74]

Machine learning and data analytics play a crucial role in decision support. They help in the rapid analysis of vast amounts of cyber security data, identifying anomalies and patterns indicative of potential threats. These disciplines bring predictive capabilities to decision support systems, enabling proactive threat mitigation.

Cyber threat intelligence is a strategic component of cyber security decision support. It provides decision-makers with information about emerging threats and vulnerabilities, allowing for informed risk assessments. Risk management, another interdisciplinary field, involves assessing the potential impact of cyber incidents and developing strategies to mitigate these risks.

The interdisciplinary nature of cyber security extends to legal and ethical dimensions. Decision-makers must navigate the legal ramifications of cyber security incidents, including data breach notifications and compliance with privacy regulations. Ethical considerations guide decision-making in addressing cyber threats while respecting individuals' rights and privacy.

Behaviourism, with its emphasis on observable behaviours and the role of conditioning in learning, can be applied metaphorically to certain aspects of cyber incident response. It is a theoretical perspective in psychology that emphasises the role of learning and observable behaviours in understanding human actions. Behaviourism can be applied to certain aspects of cyber incident response as it emphasises the role of environmental factors in influencing behaviour to the near exclusion of innate or inherited factors. By understanding the psychological levers that are pulled to dupe victims, we can better prepare for cyber security threats and mitigate the risks associated with them, including:[75]

1. The importance of conditioning and reinforcement in shaping behaviour. In the context of cyber incident response, organisations can apply this concept to training their response teams. Regular training and simulations can condition responders to react effectively to cyber incidents. Positive reinforcement through recognition or rewards for successful responses can motivate and reinforce desired behaviours.

2. Stimulus-response associations, where a specific stimulus triggers a particular response. In cyber security, organisations can establish predefined response protocols (responses) to specific cyber incident indicators (stimuli). For example, when a particular malware signature is detected (stimulus), an automated response is triggered to isolate the infected system (response).

3. Observing and analysing behaviour to understand its causes and effects. In cyber incident response, security analysts and incident responders analyse the behaviour of malware, attackers, and compromised systems to determine the nature of the threat and formulate an effective response strategy.

4. The concept of operant conditioning, where behaviours are modified through reinforcement. In the context of cyber incident response, organisations can use feedback and lessons learned from past

incidents to reinforce effective response strategies and discourage ineffective ones. This can lead to continuous improvement in incident response capabilities.

5. A focus on conditioning and learning is relevant to user training and awareness in cyber security. Organisations can use behaviourist principles to design effective security awareness programs, where users are conditioned to recognise and respond appropriately to security threats and best practices.

Research[76] into the evolving landscape of cyber security incident response delves into the architecture designed to bolster incident response capabilities. The authors introduce a cyber security architecture that comprises several essential components, each contributing to the overarching goal of enhancing incident response. The architecture incorporates threat intelligence, network monitoring, and automated response mechanisms, creating a holistic approach to incident detection and mitigation. These components work synergistically to enable proactive threat identification and immediate response, a crucial aspect of modern cyber security.

They emphasise the pivotal role of threat intelligence within the proposed architecture. Threat intelligence feeds continuously provide up-to-date information about emerging cyber threats and vulnerabilities. This timely and contextual information enables organisations to anticipate and prepare for potential incidents, ultimately reducing response time. The incorporation of threat intelligence reflects the proactive stance of the architecture, shifting from a reactive to a predictive security approach.

One of the features of the architecture is the emphasis on automated response mechanisms. In today's threat landscape, cyber attacks can unfold rapidly, leaving little time for manual intervention. The article underscores the need for automated incident response, allowing the system to execute predefined actions based on identified threats. This automation not only accelerates response times but also minimises the potential for human error.

While automation is a critical component, the research recognises the continued importance of human decision-makers in incident response. The architecture provides a framework for human intervention when necessary, ensuring that critical decisions align with organisational policies and compliance requirements. This balanced approach acknowledges that incident response is not solely a technical challenge but also a cognitive one, involving human judgment and decision-making.

Ad discussed previously, the interaction between technical and non-technical personnel during a cyber incident response can be a complex process, and several key issues related to stress can arise. Consideration needs to be given to:

1. Technical experts often use specialised terminology that non-technical staff may not understand. This can lead to misunderstandings, misinterpretations, and increased stress during critical incident discussions.

2. Technical personnel may provide an overwhelming amount of technical details and data, which can be stressful for non-technical individuals trying to grasp the situation. Processing large volumes of technical information quickly can lead to cognitive overload.

3. Cyber incident response requires rapid decision-making. Non-technical staff may feel pressured to make decisions quickly based on technical recommendations, increasing stress levels.

4. Stress can arise from the weight of responsibility and accountability during an incident. Non-technical individuals may feel anxious about their decisions' potential consequences, especially if they lack technical expertise.

5. It may be unclear who is responsible for what during an incident, leading to role ambiguity and potential conflicts. This lack of clarity can generate stress and hinder effective coordination.

6. Stressful incidents can evoke strong emotional responses, which may vary among team members. Managing emotions and reactions during high-pressure situations can be challenging, particularly for non-technical staff who may be less accustomed to such stressors.

7. Technical and non-technical team members may have differing opinions on how to respond to an incident. These disagreements can result in conflicts and increased stress levels.

8. Deciding how to allocate resources, such as personnel, time, and budget, can be a source of tension. Technical experts may prioritise technical solutions, while non-technical personnel may prioritise communication and public relations efforts.

9. Non-technical team members may not have received sufficient training or preparedness for cyber incident

response. This lack of readiness can increase stress during an incident.

10. Stressful situations can strain interpersonal relationships within the response team. It's essential to maintain effective teamwork and collaboration despite the pressure.

11. Non-technical personnel may question their technical counterparts' recommendations, leading to doubt and uncertainty. This lack of confidence can exacerbate stress.

To address these issues, organisations can implement strategies such as cross-training, clear incident response protocols, effective communication plans, and regular tabletop exercises involving both technical and non-technical staff. Additionally, recognising the potential stressors and providing support mechanisms, such as stress management training and access to mental health resources, can help mitigate the negative impacts of stress during cyber incident response efforts.

Addressing the key issues that arise when technical and non-technical personnel interact during a cyber incident response requires a combination of proactive strategies and effective communication. This may include:

1. Establish clear and open lines of communication between technical and non-technical teams. Ensure that technical experts can explain complex technical concepts in non-technical terms, fostering better understanding.

2. Encourage the use of a common language that both technical and non-technical staff can understand.

This may involve creating a shared glossary of terms used during incidents.

3. Provide training and awareness programs for non-technical personnel to familiarise them with basic cyber security concepts, incident response protocols, and common technical terminology.

4. Develop well-documented incident response plans that outline roles, responsibilities, and communication procedures for both technical and non-technical teams. Ensure that these plans are easily accessible and regularly updated.

5. Conduct tabletop exercises and simulations that involve both technical and non-technical staff. These exercises help team members practice their roles, improve communication, and identify areas for improvement.

6. Encourage cross-training between technical and non-technical teams. This can help both groups gain a better understanding of each other's roles and challenges.

7. Appoint experienced incident leaders who can bridge the gap between technical and non-technical teams. These leaders should have strong communication skills and the ability to translate technical information for non-technical stakeholders.

8. Establish a decision-making framework that considers both technical recommendations and non-technical factors, such as legal, public relations, and business impacts. Ensure that all team members understand this framework.

9. Clearly define roles and responsibilities for each team member, ensuring that everyone understands their role in the incident response process.

10. Recognise the emotional impact of cyber incidents. Provide resources and support for managing stress, anxiety, and emotional responses. This may include access to counselling or psychological support services.

11. Encourage regular feedback and debriefing sessions after incidents to identify areas for improvement in communication, coordination, and decision-making.

12. Use post-incident reviews to identify lessons learned and update incident response plans and training programs accordingly.

13. Implement collaboration and incident management tools that facilitate communication and information sharing between technical and non-technical teams.

14. Foster a culture of collaboration and mutual respect between technical and non-technical staff. Encourage a shared sense of responsibility for incident response outcomes.

15. Consider engaging external experts or consultants with experience in incident response to provide guidance and support during critical incidents.

Addressing these issues requires a holistic approach that combines technical and non-technical expertise, effective communication, and a commitment to continuous improvement. By bridging the gap between technical and non-technical teams, organisations can enhance their cyber incident response capabilities and reduce the impact of cyber threats.

Stakeholder Management

Stakeholder management is the process of identifying, analysing, engaging, and managing internal and external individuals and organisations to achieve a successful outcome. It involves understanding their interests and expectations and creating strategies to exceed them. A stakeholder may be an individual, group, or organisation that is impacted by the outcome of a business venture or project.

Stakeholders play a crucial role in managing cyber security risks. They can help lead cyber security efforts effectively by aligning business initiatives and cyber security efforts. It is important to communicate the authority of these roles and individuals to the entire constituency of expected responders and stakeholders as part of any response action plan development and training activities.

Internal and external stakeholders play a crucial role in managing cyber security risks. They can help lead cyber security efforts effectively by aligning business initiatives and cyber security efforts. It is important to communicate the authority of these roles and individuals to the entire constituency of expected responders and stakeholders as part of the emergency action plan development and training activities.

The first employees to observe indicators of malicious activities and identify cyber attacks must be empowered to make decisions quickly and without concern for any possible negative outcomes of their actions, which would inevitably delay their decision-making.

It is essential to have a cyber incident response plan that outlines an organisation's approach to prevention, preparedness, detection, response, recovery, review, and improvement. The incident response team should establish solid relationships with all the key parts of the organisation.

When asked "How well-prepared do you feel your organisation is to effectively engage with internal stakeholders during a cyber security incident?", 40% answered 'moderately well', whilst an additional 27% answered 'very well'. This is a pleasing result with the appearance that a majority of respondents being prepared for internal dialogue should a cyber attack occur. Having said that, 41% of respondents stated affirmatively when asked "Have you ever encountered challenges or difficulties in coordinating and aligning with internal stakeholders during a cyber security incident?". A higher figure, 43%, stated they were 'unsure' if there had been any difficulties. This aspect should be analysed during both cyber incident exercising (discussed later) and in post-operational assessments.

These two survey responses highlight the gulf between those respondents who think they are well prepared with regards to internal stakeholders and those who have actually gone through the process of a cyber incident and dealt with internal stakeholders.

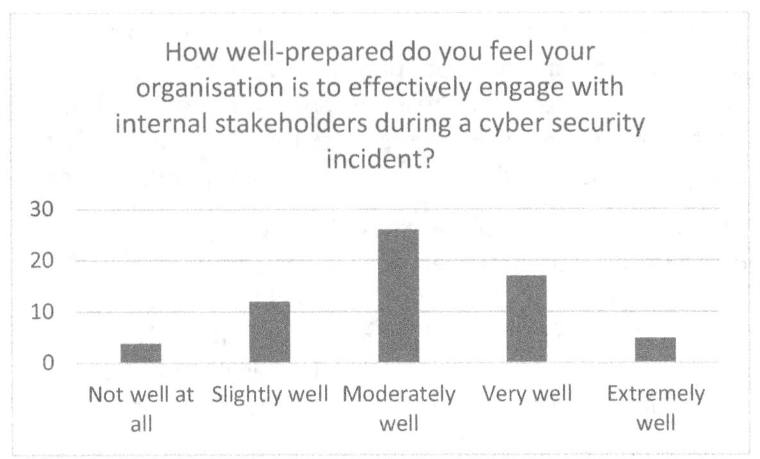

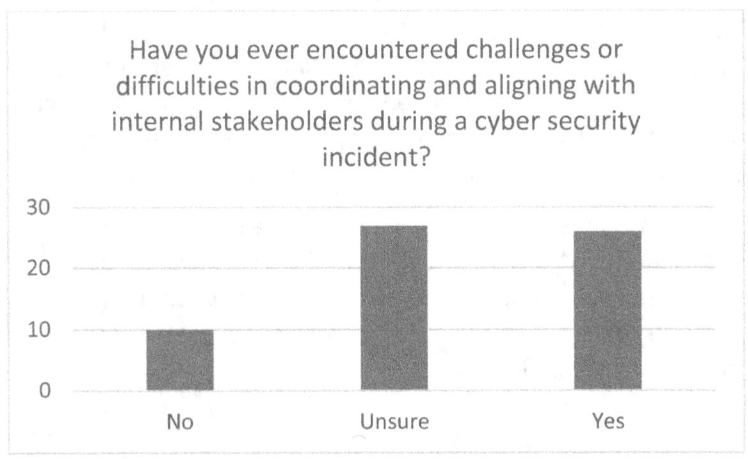

It was a different matter when survey respondents were asked "Have you ever encountered challenges or difficulties in coordinating and aligning with external stakeholders (e.g., regulators, law enforcement) during a cyber security incident?" with 55% stating 'yes'. A little over one-third were 'unsure' meaning some external stakeholders probably need to be better in articulating their requirements when informed of a cyber incident.

Additionally, when asked "How well do you feel your organisation manages the expectations and demands of external stakeholders during a cyber security incident?" 39% of survey respondents stated 'moderately well', with 27% stating 'very well'. One survey respondent commented "Who knows what their expectations are". An interesting set of responses, with respondents stating they encountered challenges or difficulties with external stakeholders, whilst at the same time considering their meeting the demands of the external stakeholders to be quite positive.

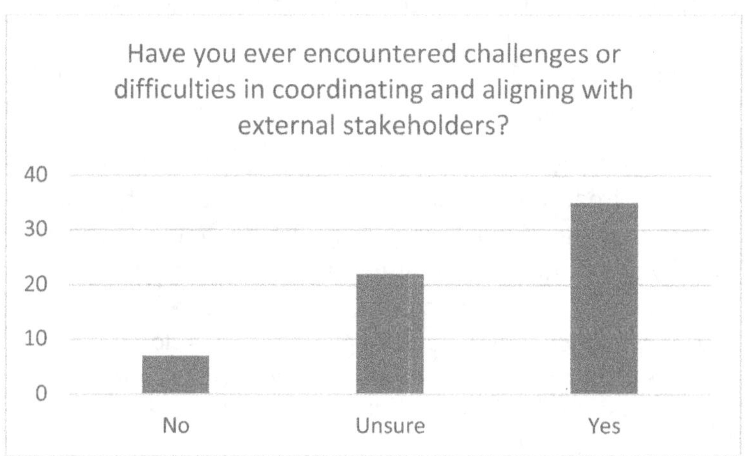

Where to Next?

The future of incident response needs to involve more advanced and automated detection and response techniques, increased collaboration between organisations and law enforcement agencies, and a greater emphasis on proactive prevention measures such as employee education and secure system design.

The future of human factors within a cyber response should include a greater emphasis on training and education (though not via shaming of employees via 'phish' testing), as well as the development of automated response systems that can help reduce the burden on human responders and improve overall response times. Additionally, there should be increased collaboration between different teams within an organisation to ensure a coordinated and effective response to ransomware attacks.

In the coming years, we can expect to see a continued emphasis on threat-intelligence, automation and artificial intelligence in incident response. Automation will allow incident responders to quickly triage and respond to incidents, while AI will enable them to more effectively analyse large amounts of data and identify patterns that may indicate a security incident.

Another trend that is likely to gain traction is the use of machine learning for incident response. Machine learning algorithms can help incident responders to detect and respond to incidents more quickly and accurately, by analysing large amounts of data and identifying patterns that may indicate a security incident.

Cloud-based incident response will also be a key trend in the future. As more and more organisations move their data and infrastructure to the cloud, incident responders will need to adapt to this new environment and develop new strategies for responding to incidents that take place in the cloud.

The use of blockchain technology may also become more prevalent in incident response. Blockchain, sometimes considered as a solution looking for a problem, can provide a secure, tamper-proof record of all incident response activities, allowing organisations to track and analyse incidents, and to demonstrate compliance with regulatory requirements. Blockchain technology can positively impact the future of cyber incident response in several ways:

1. Immutable Record Keeping: Blockchain's immutable ledger ensures that once data is recorded, it cannot be altered. This feature can be leveraged to create a tamper-proof record of incident response actions, preserving the integrity of digital evidence. Incident

response teams can use blockchain to securely document their activities, helping in investigations and compliance audits.

2. Secure Data Sharing: Blockchain can enable secure and auditable data sharing among incident response teams, organisations, and even across industries. Information about threats, attack patterns, and indicators of compromise can be shared in real-time, enhancing collective defence against cyber threats.

3. Decentralised Authentication: Blockchain-based authentication can enhance the security of incident response processes. Decentralised identity verification systems can reduce the risk of identity theft or impersonation during incident response coordination, ensuring that only authorised individuals access sensitive information.

4. Smart Contracts for Automated Response: Smart contracts on blockchain platforms can automate incident response actions based on predefined criteria. For example, when specific threat indicators are detected, a smart contract can trigger automated responses such as isolating compromised systems or initiating a predefined incident response plan.

5. Tokenised Credentials: Blockchain can be used to create and manage digital credentials securely. Incident responders can hold verifiable credentials that attest to their skills and certifications, reducing the risk of credential fraud within response teams.

6. Supply Chain Security: Blockchain technology can be applied to supply chain security, ensuring the integrity of software and hardware components used

in incident response. This reduces the risk of compromised tools or equipment that could hinder response efforts.

7. Resilience to DDoS Attacks: Some blockchain networks may be resistant to DDoS attacks due to their decentralised nature. Incident response systems hosted on such blockchains may remain operational during DDoS attacks, ensuring continuous response capabilities.

8. Data Provenance and Chain of Custody: Blockchain can provide an immutable record of data provenance and chain of custody for digital evidence. This is critical in maintaining the integrity of evidence collected during cyber incident investigations, supporting legal proceedings.

9. Privacy-Preserving Incident Reporting: Blockchain can facilitate anonymous or pseudonymous incident reporting, encouraging individuals or organisations to share information about security incidents without revealing sensitive details. This can lead to a more open and collaborative incident response environment.

10. Improved Threat Intelligence Sharing: Blockchain can enhance the security and trustworthiness of threat intelligence sharing platforms. Threat indicators and intelligence data shared through blockchain networks are less susceptible to manipulation or falsification, promoting trust among participants.

Incorporating blockchain technology into cyber incident response processes requires careful planning and consideration of specific use cases. While blockchain offers significant advantages, it's essential to address scalability, interoperability, and regulatory challenges to fully harness its potential in incident response. As the technology matures and standards emerge, its role in enhancing cyber incident response capabilities may grow. Whilst using blockchain for incident response many be an overkill at current time, in future it could benefit from blockchain. Who knows what the future may hold.

As cyber threats continue to evolve, incident response teams will also have to adapt to new types of attacks. Ransomware and supply chain attacks are becoming more common, and incident responders will need to develop new strategies to detect and respond to these types of incidents.

Artificial intelligence (AI) is rapidly becoming an important tool in the fight against cyber threats, including incident response. AI-based technologies can be used in various stages of incident response, including detection, analysis, and recovery.

1. Detection: AI can be used to detect cyber incidents in real-time by analysing network traffic and identifying abnormal patterns or behaviour that indicate a potential attack. This can include identifying malware, phishing attempts, and other malicious activity. Additionally, AI can also be used to monitor user behaviour, such as detecting suspicious login attempts, and can flag potential incidents for further investigation.

2. Analysis: AI can be used to analyse large amounts of data generated by network and security devices, such as firewall logs and intrusion detection systems. This can help incident responders quickly identify the

scope and nature of an attack, as well as the systems and data that have been affected.

3. Recovery: AI can be used to assist in the recovery process by automating tasks such as isolating and containing infected systems, and restoring backups. This can speed up the recovery process and minimise the disruption caused by a cyber incident.

4. Predictive analysis: AI can also be used to analyse historical data to predict future attacks. This can help organisations proactively identify and mitigate potential vulnerabilities and threats.

5. Virtual assistance: AI can also be used to provide virtual assistance to incident responders, such as providing automated guidance on steps to be taken, and performing actions such as isolating compromised systems.

6. Automated incident response: AI can also be used to automate incident response actions, such as quarantining compromised systems, restoring backups, and escalating incidents to human incident responders.

7. Cyber threat intelligence: AI can also be used to analyse cyber threat intelligence data and provide insights into the tactics, techniques, and procedures used by attackers. This can help incident responders understand the nature of the attack and make more informed decisions on how to respond.

8. Continuous monitoring: AI-based systems can be used to continuously monitor the network and provide real-time alerts of any suspicious activity.

This can help organisations quickly detect and respond to cyber incidents, minimising the impact and damage.

However, it's important to note that AI-based systems require proper configuration and maintenance to be effective, and in some cases, they may generate false positives or negatives. Additionally, AI-based incident response systems may require significant resources and expertise to implement and maintain, which can be a challenge for some organisations.

Humanitarian Assistance

When considering the impact of cyber incident response upon first responders, the organisations they work for, and that of the impacted individuals, we could draw parallels with humanitarian assistance. Humanitarian assistance refers to the provision of aid and support to individuals and communities affected by natural disasters, armed conflicts, or other crises. This aid can take many forms, including food, shelter, medical care, and other basic necessities.

Humanitarian assistance as its own sector has been in existence for many decades. The lessons learnt from the many deployments, often provided in dangerous and difficult surroundings could be beneficial in supporting cyber incident responders. Responding to a humanitarian disaster and responding to a cyber-attack have several similarities, including:

1. Rapid response: In both cases, a rapid response is crucial to minimise damage and save lives. In the case of a humanitarian disaster, emergency responders must quickly assess the situation and take action to provide aid and assistance. In the case of a cyber-attack, organisations must quickly detect and respond to the attack to minimise damage and protect sensitive information.

2. Coordination and collaboration: Both types of response efforts require coordination and collaboration among multiple stakeholders, including government agencies, non-profit organisations, and private sector companies.

3. Risk assessment: In both cases, it is important to assess the risks and potential impacts of the event in order to prioritise response efforts and allocate resources appropriately.

4. Communication: Effective communication is essential for both types of response efforts. In the case of a humanitarian disaster, communication is needed to coordinate response efforts and provide information to the public. In the case of a cyber-attack, communication is needed to notify affected parties and provide guidance on how to respond.

5. Recovery: Both types of events require recovery efforts to restore normal operations and help affected individuals and communities return to their pre-disaster state.

6. Preparedness: Preparedness is key in both cases, both in terms of having a plan and the necessary resources in place before an event occurs, as well as

    in terms of ongoing training and readiness activities to be prepared to respond effectively.

7. Continuity of operations: In both cases, the ability to maintain continuity of operations is important to ensure that essential services can continue to be provided even in the face of the event.

8. International dimension: Both types of disasters can have international dimensions, requiring coordination and cooperation with other countries and organisations.

Individuals who respond to a humanitarian crisis, such as aid workers, first responders, and volunteers, may experience a wide range of psychological impacts because of their work. Specifically, the constant stress and demands of responding to a crisis can lead to feelings of exhaustion, cynicism, and a lack of motivation. This can affect an individual's ability to perform their job effectively and may lead them to leaving the industry.

Communication and Collaboration

Responsibilities of Government:

Government agencies hold several responsibilities when it comes to assisting organisations during cyber attacks. Primarily, they are tasked with establishing and enforcing cyber security regulations and potential standards, ensuring that organisations adhere to best practices for prevention, detection, and response to cyber threats. Regulators also monitor compliance, conduct audits, and impose penalties for non-compliance, incentivising organisations to prioritise cyber security.

When asked "How would you rate the level of collaboration and communication between your organisation and external stakeholders (e.g., regulators, law enforcement) during a cyber security incident?", 35% of survey respondents stated 'average', followed by 25% stating 'good'. Unfortunately, 11% of survey respondents stating the level of collaboration and communication was 'very poor'.

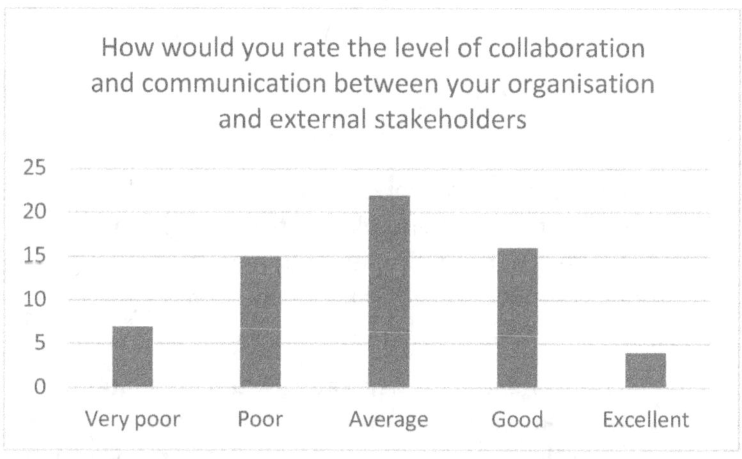

When asked "How satisfied are you with the support and guidance provided by regulators and industry bodies during a cyber security incident?" 28% of survey respondents were 'neither satisfied or unsatisfied', followed by 27% being 'moderately satisfied'. These responses were quite level across most categories, with 19% being 'extremely dissatisfied'.

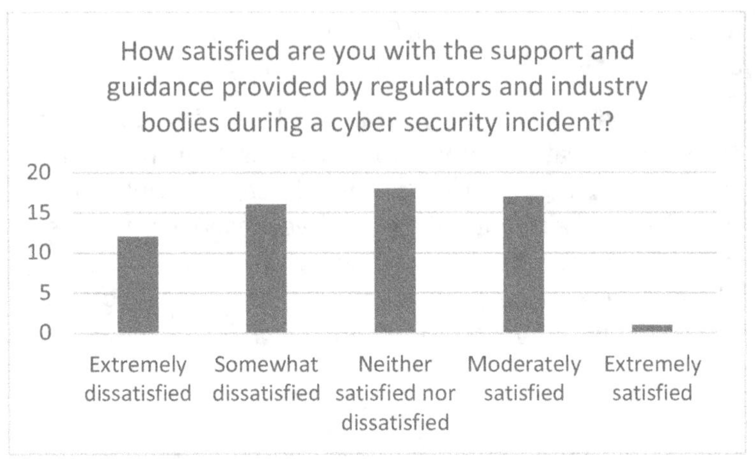

Strategies Employed by Government Regulators:

1. Regulatory Frameworks: Government regulators create and update regulatory frameworks that outline cyber security requirements for organisations. These frameworks serve as guidelines for building robust cyber resilience.

2. Incident Reporting: Regulators often mandate that organisations report cyber security incidents promptly. This allows regulators to assess the scope and impact of incidents and provide assistance as needed.

3. Coordination with Law Enforcement: Government regulators collaborate with law enforcement agencies to investigate cybercriminal activities. They provide information to aid in the identification and apprehension of threat actors, which can deter future attacks.

4. Information Sharing: Regulators facilitate information sharing among organisations and sectors. Sharing threat intelligence and best practices enhances collective defence against cyber threats.

5. Incident Response Planning: Regulators encourage organisations to develop comprehensive incident response plans. They may provide guidelines and conduct exercises to ensure that organisations are well-prepared to respond effectively.

Impact of Government Regulators: The impact of government regulators in assisting organisations during cyber attacks is significant. Their actions should contribute to:

1. Improved Cyber Resilience: Regulatory frameworks and enforcement drive organisations to invest in cyber security measures, ultimately bolstering their resilience against cyber threats.

2. Enhanced Incident Response: Regulators' emphasis on incident reporting and response planning ensures that organisations can mitigate the impact of cyber attacks more effectively.

3. Legal Accountability: Regulators often hold organisations accountable for data breaches and non-compliance with cyber security regulations, discouraging negligence in cyber security practices.

4. Deterrence: The prospect of regulatory penalties and legal consequences may motivate organisations to prioritise cyber security.

5. Collaborative Ecosystem: Government regulators foster collaboration within the cyber security ecosystem, leading to the development of stronger

defences and a more united front against cyber threats.

Responsibilities of Law Enforcement:

Law enforcement agencies shoulder several critical responsibilities in assisting organisations during cyber attacks. These responsibilities include:

1. Investigation: Law enforcement agencies are responsible for investigating cyber attacks, identifying the perpetrators, and gathering evidence to build cases against cybercriminals. This investigative work is vital for bringing cyber criminals to justice.

2. Evidence Preservation: Law enforcement helps organisations preserve digital evidence related to the cyber-attack. This evidence is crucial for both investigations and potential legal proceedings.

3. Threat Attribution: Determining the origin and attribution of cyber attacks is essential for understanding the motive behind the attack and the potential threat actors involved. Law enforcement agencies use their resources to track and attribute cyber attacks.

4. Collaboration: Law enforcement collaborates with other organisations, such as computer emergency response teams, to share threat intelligence and mitigation strategies. This collaboration enhances the overall response to cyber threats.

Strategies Employed by Law Enforcement: Law enforcement agencies employ various strategies to assist organisations during cyber attacks:

1. Cybercrime Units: Many law enforcement agencies have specialised cybercrime units staffed with experts in digital forensics, cyber security, and computer crime. These units are dedicated to handling cyber-attack cases.

2. Public Awareness: Law enforcement agencies often engage in public awareness campaigns to educate organisations and individuals about cyber threats and best practices for prevention and response.

3. Partnerships: They should establish partnerships with organisations, including private sector entities and international law enforcement agencies, to share information, resources, and expertise in combatting cybercrime.

4. Cybercrime Legislation: Law enforcement works with legislatures to draft and enact cybercrime legislation that empowers authorities to investigate and prosecute cyber criminals effectively.

Impact of Law Enforcement: The impact of law enforcement in assisting organisations during cyber attacks should include:

1. Deterrence: The knowledge that law enforcement is actively investigating cybercrimes serves as a deterrent to potential attackers.

2. Justice: Law enforcement's investigative efforts can lead to the identification, apprehension, and prosecution of cybercriminals, ensuring they face legal consequences.

3. Prevention and Preparedness: Organisations are encouraged to invest in cyber security measures and incident response plans to prevent future attacks and be better prepared to respond.

4. Resource Sharing: Law enforcement agencies share valuable threat intelligence, helping organisations understand emerging threats and vulnerabilities.

5. International Cooperation: In an interconnected world, law enforcement's international cooperation is vital in addressing cross-border cybercrime, bringing cybercriminals to justice, and dismantling cybercriminal networks.

When asked "How important do you think it is for your organisation to establish strong relationships with external stakeholders (e.g., regulators, law enforcement) for effective incident response?", unsurprisingly, 38% stated 'extremely important' whilst a further 38% stated 'very important'.

However, when asked "How satisfied are you with the level of support and assistance provided by law enforcement agencies during a cyber security incident?", 28% of survey respondents stated 'neither satisfied or unsatisfied, followed by 18% stating they were 'somewhat dissatisfied', whilst an additional 17% stated they were 'extremely dissatisfied'. These figures do not surprise me and follow a trend of other research I have conducted. If there is one significant area where incident response can be greatly improved, it is the ability of law enforcement agencies to play a more active and purposeful role.

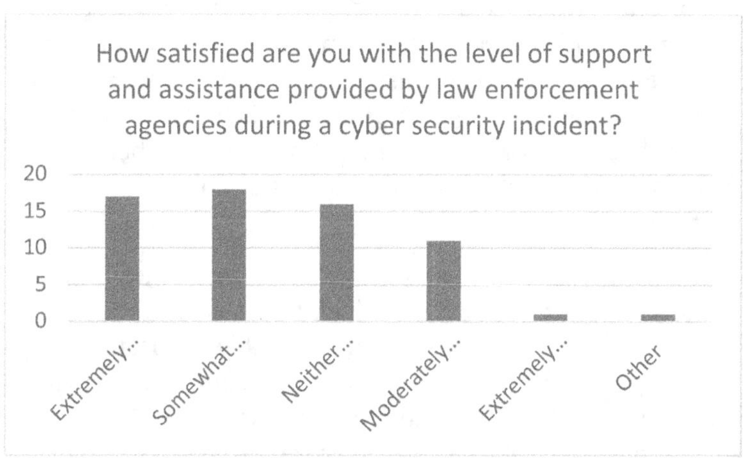

The Impact on Individuals

Cyber attacks can have a wide range of social and psychological impacts on individuals if they become victims to online crime, including feelings of violation, loss of trust, and anxiety. It is important to understand the social and psychological impact of cyber attacks and developing strategies to mitigate these impacts. By doing so, we can help to minimise the negative consequences of cyber attacks and promote a more resilient and secure society.

Cyber security is a field that has become increasingly important in recent years. With the rise of cyber attacks, companies and governments are investing more resources into protecting their digital assets. However, working in cyber security can be challenging, both mentally and emotionally. A study[77] has shown early evidence of burnout in cyber professionals, signalling a potential loss of skills to a critical part of the economy.

One of the most significant psychological challenges of working in cyber security is the high-stress environment. Cyber security professionals are responsible for protecting their organisation's digital assets from cyber attacks and in doing so, must be vigilant and proactive in identifying and mitigating potential threats. This constant pressure can lead to high levels of stress and anxiety, which can have negative effects on mental health. A study[78] in 2021 found 51% of cyber security professionals experienced extreme stress or burnout due to their jobs.

Burnout, as discussed earlier, is another psychological challenge that cyber security professionals face. Burnout is a state of emotional, physical, and mental exhaustion caused by prolonged exposure to stress. Cyber security professionals may be required to work long hours and be on sometimes be on call 24/7. This can lead to burnout, which can have serious consequences for both the individual and the organisation. It is essential for organisations to recognise these challenges and provide their cyber security teams with the support they need to do their jobs effectively.

Another psychological challenge that cyber security professionals face can be a lack of resources. Cyber security is a field that is constantly evolving, and professionals must stay up to date with the latest threats and technologies. However, many organisations do not provide their cyber security teams with the resources they need to do their jobs effectively. This can lead to frustration and exhaustion.[79]

When asked "To what extent does responding to a cyber security incident make you feel vulnerable or at risk?" 42% said 'slightly' whilst 24% responded as 'moderately'. When asked "How anxious or fearful do you typically feel when responding to a cyber security incident?" 34% stated 'slightly' whilst 23% said 'very' anxious or fearful.

Further research needs to be undertaken to unpack these results, however some parallels can be drawn with police and emergency service workers. A survey[80] which studied the mental health and wellbeing of more than 21,000 police and emergency services workers and volunteers found that these workers are more than twice as likely to experience high or very high rates of psychological distress compared to the general population. It also found that employees who had worked more than 10 years were almost twice as likely to experience psychological distress and were six times more likely to experience symptoms of post-traumatic stress disorder.

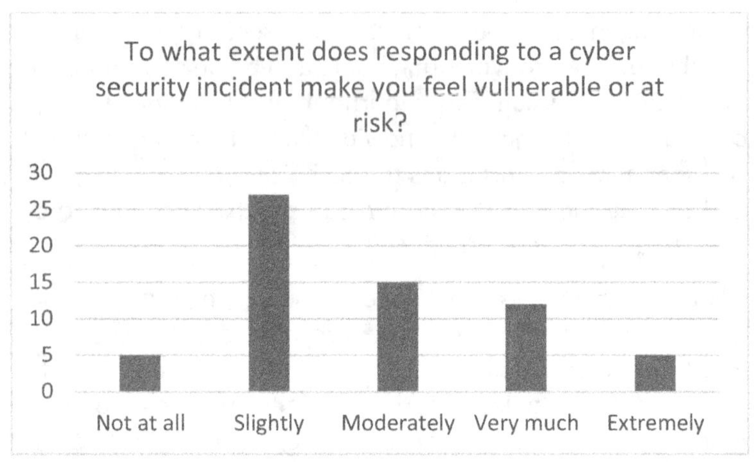

To what extent does responding to a cyber security incident make you feel vulnerable or at risk?
30
25
20
15
10
5
0
Not at all
Slightly
Moderately
Very much
Extremely

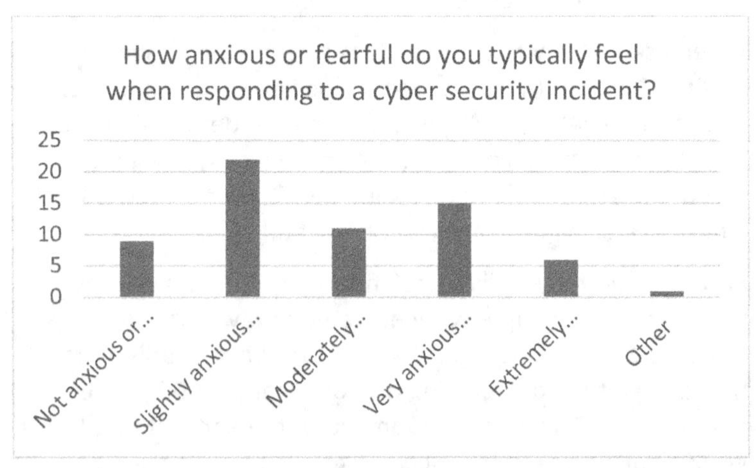

How anxious or fearful do you typically feel when responding to a cyber security incident?
25
20
15
10
5
0
Not anxious or...
Slightly anxious...
Moderately...
Very anxious...
Extremely...
Other

Cybercrime can impact individuals who might be the victims of a cybercrime – such as such as children, the elderly, and those with mental health issues – as well as the individuals who are responding to a cybercrime. This can be amplified by the media, which can increase public anxiety and create a sense of panic. For example, a victim of a phishing attack may feel violated that their personal information has been stolen, while a victim of a denial-of-service attack may feel anxious about the disruption to their daily routine.

Cyber attacks can be particularly significant for vulnerable individuals or groups, such as children, the elderly, and those with mental health issues. For example, a child who has been the victim of cyberbullying may experience significant emotional distress, while an elderly person who has fallen victim to a scam may feel vulnerable and isolated. There is also the impact of cyber attacks on organisations. This can include financial losses, reputational damage, and legal liabilities. For example, a company that suffers a data breach may incur significant costs in terms of data recovery, compensation to affected customers, and legal fees.[81]

It is important to take a proactive approach to mitigate the impacts of cyber attacks on vulnerable individuals or groups, such as children, the elderly, and those with mental health issues. This may include:[82]

- Providing clear and accurate information about the nature and scope of the cyber attack, including advice on how to protect personal information and prevent further harm.

- Offering emotional support in the aftermath of a cyber attack. This could include counselling or therapy services, as well as support from family and friends.

- Increasing cyber security awareness by educating vulnerable individuals or groups about the risks of cyber attacks and how to prevent them.

- Developing tailored incident response plans which consider the needs of vulnerable individuals or groups.

- Providing training and support to caregivers, such as parents or healthcare providers, to help them protect vulnerable individuals or groups from cyber attacks and provide support in the aftermath of an incident.

There are various strategies that can be employed to mitigate the social and psychological impact of a cyber incident, including providing support and information to affected individuals, increasing cyber security awareness, and developing effective incident response plans. A multi-pronged approach is necessary to effectively mitigate the social and psychological impacts of cybercrime. This includes:[83]

- Providing support and information to affected individuals about the nature and scope of the attack, and offering advice on how to protect personal information.

- Increasing cyber security awareness by educating individuals about the risks of cyber attacks and how to prevent them, can reduce the likelihood of people becoming victims of cybercrime, and reduce the impact when attacks do occur.

- Developing effective incident response plans for responding to cyber attacks can help organisations to mitigate the impact of an attack and minimise the risk of future attacks.

- Implementing technological solutions such as encryption and firewalls can help to reduce the risk of cyber attacks and protect personal and sensitive information.

- Collaborating with other organisations by sharing information about cyber threats and attacks, organisations can work together to develop more effective cyber security measures and improve their incident response capabilities.

A study[84] which focused on the different coping strategies used by individuals who have been victims of cybercrime discovered that individuals who use active coping strategies, such as seeking social support or engaging in problem-solving, will experience less psychological distress than those who use avoidant coping strategies, such as denial or disengagement. The study also found that the type of cyber victimisation experienced was related to the level of psychological distress. Participants who experienced identity theft or financial fraud reported higher levels of psychological distress than those who experienced other types of cyber victimisation, such as cyber stalking or harassment.

Another study[85] of existing research on the psychological impact of cybercrime including hacking, phishing, identity theft, and cyber stalking, found victims suffered common psychological effects including anxiety, depression, post-traumatic stress disorder, and social isolation. In addition, victims of cybercrime were found to have higher levels of psychological distress than victims of traditional crime.

The factors that influenced the psychological impact of cybercrime on victims included the severity and duration of the cybercrime, the level of personal investment in the online activity that was targeted, and the victim's coping mechanisms.

The authors highlight the importance of providing support for victims of cybercrime to help them manage the psychological impact of the experience. They suggest victim support services should be tailored to the specific needs of cybercrime victims, and that interventions should focus on reducing feelings of isolation and anxiety.

When asked "Do you feel that your organisation provides adequate training and resources to help you cope with the stress encountered during a cyber security incident?", 30% or survey respondents stated 'somewhat inadequate', whilst 24% stated 'neither adequate nor inadequate'. Somewhat disappointingly, and proving we have a long way yet to go, 17% reported their training and resources was 'extremely inadequate'.

When asked "How often do you perceive responding to a cyber security incident as an opportunity for growth and development?", 40% of survey respondents stated 'most of the time', whilst 31% stated 'always'.

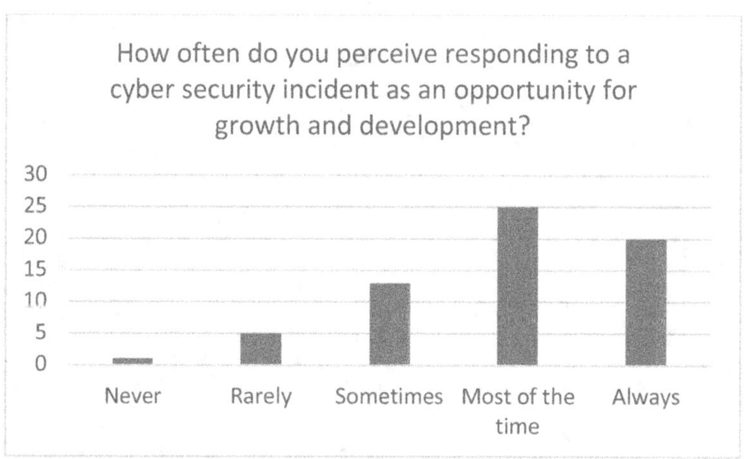

When asked "To what extent does responding to a cyber security incident motivate you to enhance your skills and knowledge?", 44% of survey respondents stated 'very much', whilst 33% stated 'extremely'. This is a pleasing response, acknowledging the high degree of motivation by survey respondents to improve their incident response skills and knowledge.

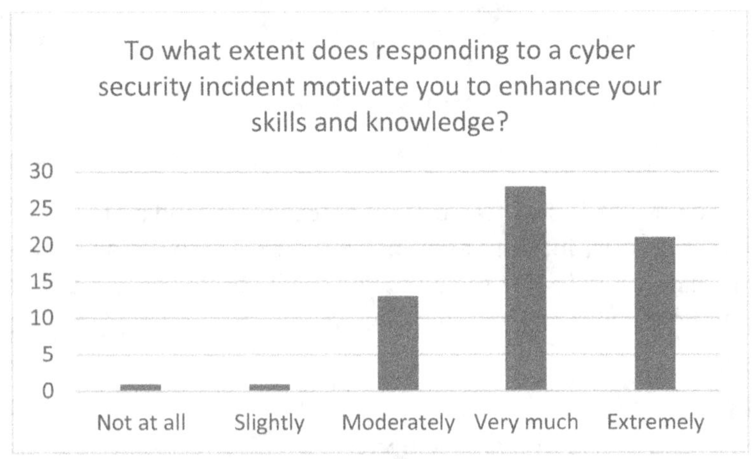

The Impact on Organisations

Cyber attacks can have a profound and lasting impact on organisations, affecting not only their financial well-being but also their reputation, customer trust, and overall operations.

One of the most immediate and tangible impacts of a cyber-attack is the financial burden it places on an organisation. This impact can be observed in various ways:

1. Financial Losses: Cyber incidents often lead to direct financial losses, including the cost of investigating the incident, restoring systems and data, and reimbursing affected parties for any losses incurred.

2. Legal and Regulatory Fines: Organisations may face fines and legal penalties for failing to protect sensitive data, especially in cases of data breaches involving personal or financial information. Regulatory bodies, such as GDPR in Europe, impose substantial fines for non-compliance.

3. Business Disruption: Cyber incidents can disrupt business operations, resulting in revenue losses due to downtime, decreased productivity, and delayed projects.

The impact of a cyber attack can extend beyond financial losses and tarnish an organisation's reputation and erode customer trust:

1. Damage to Brand Image: A cyber incident can damage an organisation's brand image, making it appear vulnerable and unreliable. Customers may lose confidence in the organisation's ability to safeguard their data.

2. Loss of Customer Trust: Customers who have their data compromised in a breach may lose trust in the organisation and take their business elsewhere. Rebuilding this trust can be a lengthy and challenging process.

Cyber attacks can disrupt an organisation's day-to-day operations, leading to various operational challenges:

1. System Downtime: Ransomware attacks or other cyber incidents can lead to extended system downtime, preventing employees from accessing critical resources and impeding workflow.

2. Loss of Intellectual Property: Theft of intellectual property through cyber espionage can hinder an organisation's innovation and competitive advantage.

3. Business Continuity: Organisations need to invest in disaster recovery and business continuity planning to mitigate the operational impact of a cyber incident.

Cyber attacks can have legal and compliance ramifications that extend beyond financial penalties:

1. Legal Action: Affected parties may pursue legal action against the organisation, seeking compensation for damages resulting from the breach.

2. Regulatory Scrutiny: Regulators may investigate the incident and impose additional compliance requirements on the organisation.

The impacts of a cyber-attack can linger long after the initial incident:

1. Increased Security Costs: Organisations often need to invest in enhanced cyber security measures, security training, and incident response capabilities to prevent future attacks, increasing their operational costs.

2. Insurance Premiums: Cyber insurance premiums may rise after an attack, as insurers perceive the organisation as a higher risk.

When asked "How confident do you feel in your organisation's ability to quickly detect and identify a cyber security incident?", 36% or survey respondents stated they were 'confident', whilst 22% stated they were 'not very confident' to detect and identify a cyber security incident. With the responses aggregated, more than a third of survey respondents had low levels of confidence in their organisations ability to detect and identify a cyber incident. This is a troubling amount.

For example, hospitals are increasingly becoming targets for ransomware attacks due to their dependence on electronic medical records and the criticality of the healthcare services they provide. Ransomware attacks on hospitals not only result in financial losses but also have a significant impact on patient care and data security.

Ransomware attacks on hospitals often lead to a disruption of medical services, with patients being turned away or treated in alternative facilities. Patient care can also be compromised due to the loss of medical records or delays in accessing patient data. Ransomware attacks on hospitals can have long-term implications for data security, as attackers can steal sensitive patient information and use it for malicious purposes such as identity theft or medical fraud.[86]

The Cost of Cybercrime

There are several factors that contribute to the cost of a cyber incident. From an incident response perspective they include the cost of recovering data, the cost of lost productivity, the cost of IT support, the cost of legal fees, and the cost of reputation damage. There are also indirect costs of a cyber-attack, such as lost productivity and reputation damage, however these can be difficult to quantify. I have previously quantified the cost of cybercrime in Australia at ~$2bn per year, or ~2% of GDP.[87]

There are various economic incentives that drive ransomware attacks, specifically the use of crypto currencies in facilitating ransomware payments. The broader anonymity and irreversibility of crypto currency transactions provide a financial incentive for cyber criminals to engage in ransomware attacks. Ransomware attacks are a profitable business for attackers, generating billions of dollars in revenue. Likewise, ransomware attacks have a significant economic impact on organisations, including direct costs of paying ransoms and indirect costs of business disruption, lost productivity, and reputational damage. Unfortunately, the cost of ransomware attacks has been increasing over time, driven by higher ransom demands and the increasing sophistication of attackers.[88]

Estimating the precise cost of a specific cybercrime can be challenging due to the numerous variables involved. For example, the costs of a ransomware attack can vary widely depending on the size of the organisation, the severity of the attack, and the ransom demands made by the attackers. There have been several studies into the monetary costs of a ransomware attack on organisations, each with various outcomes. The wide variance in amounts highlights how difficult it is to accurately cost cybercrime:

1. The average cost of cybercrime per report during 2022/23 was up 14 per cent from the previous year. This included: small business $46,000; medium business $97,200; and large business $71,600.[89]

2. It is estimated that there is a ransomware attack on a business every 11 seconds on average, with global ransomware damage losses projected to reach $20 billion.[90]

3. The average cost of a data breach for businesses with fewer than 500 employees is USD 2.98 million, and the average cost per breached record is USD 164.[91]

4. The average cost of a ransomware attack was between $1,000 and $700,000, with a median cost of $10,000.[92]

5. The average ransom demand was $170,404, while the average actual payment was $154,108, with the estimated that the total cost of ransomware attacks in 2020 was $20 billion.[93]

6. The average cost of a ransomware attack was approximately €43,000, with a range of €3,000 to €1.5 million.[94]

7. The global average cost of a data breach in 2023 was USD 4.45 million, which is a 15% increase over the past 3 years.[95]

The largest cost of a ransomware attack is typically associated with the interruption of business operations, which accounted for approximately 50% of the total cost. The cost of data recovery and remediation accounted for approximately 30% of the total cost, while the cost of reputational damage accounted for approximately 20%. The cost of a ransomware attack varies depending on the size of the organisation and the type of data that was targeted. Small businesses were found to be particularly vulnerable to the cost of a ransomware attack, as they often lacked the resources to quickly recover from an attack.[96]

Competent and fast incident response is crucial for organisations to mitigate the financial and temporal impact of a cyber attack. When a security incident occurs, swift and efficient response can significantly reduce the time it takes to identify, contain, and eradicate the threat. The faster an organisation can detect and respond to a cyber attack, the less time the attacker has to compromise systems, steal sensitive data, or cause disruption. This rapid response not only limits the extent of the damage but also minimises the potential financial losses associated with data breaches, system downtime, and reputational damage.

Moreover, a well-executed incident response plan helps organisations save money by streamlining the recovery process. A prompt and effective response helps in isolating the affected systems, restoring services, and implementing security measures to prevent future incidents. This limits the impact on productivity and revenue, reducing the overall cost of recovery. Additionally, organisations with robust incident response capabilities are better positioned to comply with regulatory requirements, avoiding potential fines and legal consequences that may arise from a lack of diligence in handling cyber security incidents. In essence, investing in competent incident response not only protects an organisation's assets and reputation but also contributes to significant cost and time savings in the aftermath of a cyber attack.

Prevention

An ounce of prevention is worth a pound of cure – Benjamin Franklin

This publication has discussed how a cyber incident can cause significant damage to an organisation's reputation, finances, and operations. Cyber attacks can lead to data breaches, which can result in the loss of sensitive information such as personal data, financial information, and intellectual property. This can lead to legal and financial consequences, as well as damage to the organisation's reputation. Additionally, cyber attacks can disrupt an organisation's operations, leading to downtime and lost productivity. By investing in cyber security prevention measures, organisations can save significant amounts of money in the long run, and maybe not have to conduct incident response.

In 2022/23 there were nearly 94,000 reports were made to the Australian Government through ReportCyber – around one every 6 minutes. My previous research has concluded such reports are only ~one-fifth of the actual cybercrimes which occur in Australia.[97] To boost cyber security, Australian organisations must consider not only technical controls such as ASD's Essential Eight, but also growing a positive cyber-secure culture across business and the community. This includes prioritising secure-by-design and secure-by-default products during both development (vendors) and procurement (customers).[98]

To prevent cyber attacks, organisations should firstly focus on basic cyber hygiene, such as training their employees on cyber attack prevention, keeping their software and systems up to date, and ensure endpoint protection, to name but a few.

Preventing a cyber attack can be a challenging task, but there are several steps that organisations can take to reduce the risk of a successful attack:

1. Back up your data: Having a recent and secure backup of your data is critical in the event of a ransomware attack. This allows you to restore your data without having to pay the ransom.

2. Keep software and systems updated: Make sure that all software and systems are up to date with the latest security patches. This will help to protect against known vulnerabilities that can be exploited by attackers.

3. Use strong passwords: Use strong and unique passwords (and more importantly, passphrases) for all accounts, and enable two-factor authentication (preferably not SMS based) where possible. This will make it more difficult for attackers to gain access to your systems.

4. Use Antivirus software: Antivirus software can help to detect and prevent malware, including ransomware, from infecting your systems. Make sure that your antivirus software is kept up-to-date and that regular scans are run.

5. Train employees: Educate your employees about the dangers of various cybercrimes and how to recognise and avoid phishing emails and other malicious links.

6. Limit access to sensitive data: Limit access to sensitive data to only those who need it, and make sure that all sensitive data is encrypted.

7. Monitor your network: Use monitoring tools to detect and respond to suspicious activity on your network, including threat intelligence. This will help you to detect an attack quickly and respond before it can cause significant damage.

8. Have an incident response plan: Having a well-defined incident response plan in place will help you to respond quickly and effectively to a ransomware attack.

9. Consider cyber insurance: Cyber insurance can help to offset the financial losses caused by a cyber attack and may also provide access to expert assistance for incident response and recovery.

It is important for organisations to prepare for a cyber incident by developing a comprehensive incident response plan. This includes:

- Incident Response Team: Form a dedicated incident response team comprising experts in cyber security, legal, communication, and public relations.

- Plan Development: Create a detailed incident response plan that outlines roles, responsibilities, and procedures for identifying, containing, and mitigating cyber threats.

- Tabletop Exercises: Regularly conduct tabletop exercises to simulate cyber incident scenarios and ensure the readiness of the incident response team.

- Communication Strategy: Establish a clear communication plan for both internal stakeholders and external entities, such as customers, partners, and regulatory authorities.

Robust data backup and recovery strategies are also essential:

- Data Backups: Regularly back up critical data, and store backups in secure, offline locations to prevent ransomware attacks.

- Disaster Recovery Plans: Develop and test disaster recovery plans to ensure timely data restoration in the event of a cyber-attack.

Limit the potential impact of a cyber incident by implementing network segmentation and access controls:

- Network Segmentation: Divide the network into isolated segments to contain an attack's spread.

- Zero Trust Model: Adopt a zero-trust approach, where access to resources is authenticated and authorised on a need-to-know basis.

Stay vigilant by leveraging threat intelligence and continuous monitoring:

- Threat Intelligence Feeds: Subscribe to threat intelligence feeds to stay informed about emerging threats.

- Security Information and Event Management (SIEM): Employ SIEM solutions to monitor network activity and detect anomalies indicative of cyber incidents.

Enforce cyber security policies and adhere to regulatory compliance requirements:

- Policy Review: Regularly review and update cyber security policies to align with evolving threats and technologies.

- Compliance Adherence: Ensure compliance with data protection regulations, industry standards, and legal requirements.

Preventing cybercrime requires a multi-layered approach that combines technical measures with employee training and incident response planning. By taking the steps outlined above (and others depending on your network and broader situation), organisations can significantly reduce their risk of falling victim to a cyber attack. Governments can play a role in mitigating the impact of cybercrime by increasing regulation and enforcement, improving incident response capabilities, and facilitating international cooperation.[99]

One aspect of prevention is the development and simulation of cyber disaster situation awareness models, which can help organisations in responding to and recovering from cyber disasters. Such simulations highlight the importance of situation awareness, which refers to the ability to perceive, understand, and project the state of a given environment.

Models which may be considered are the Cyberattack Severity Model (CSM) and the Cyberattack Situation Awareness Model (CSAM). The CSM is designed to assess the severity of cyber attacks by considering several factors, including the impact on assets, the sophistication of the attack, and the potential for future attacks. The CSAM, on the other hand, provides a framework for improving situation awareness during cyber disasters by providing real-time monitoring and decision support.[100]

The CSM is a framework used to assess the potential impact of a cyber-attack on an organisation. It is a way of categorising cyber attacks based on their level of severity and the potential damage they could cause.

The model typically considers several factors, including the type of attack, the target of the attack, the potential loss of data or intellectual property, and the impact on the organisation's reputation, revenue, and operations.

The severity model can be used to help organisations prioritise their cyber security efforts and allocate resources to address the most significant threats. It can also be useful for risk assessment and incident response planning.

There are several different severity models in use, but they generally involve some form of rating system that assigns a score or level of severity to each type of cyber attack. These ratings may be based on factors such as the attack's complexity, the potential harm to the organisation, and the likelihood of the attack being successful.

Consideration may include:

1. Collecting and analysing data from various sources to detect potential cyber threats.

2. Using tools and techniques to analyse the data and identify potential threats and vulnerabilities.

3. Evaluating the potential impact of the threats and vulnerabilities on the organisation's operations and assets.

4. Developing and implementing appropriate strategies to respond to the threats and vulnerabilities.

5. Communicating the status of the cyber security posture to relevant stakeholders and sharing information on potential threats and vulnerabilities.

Training & Education

Training cyber incident responders is crucial to ensure that organisations can respond effectively to cyber attacks. Cyber security threats are constantly evolving, and attackers are becoming more sophisticated in their methods. Therefore, it is essential for organisations to have a well-trained team of cyber incident responders who can identify, contain, and mitigate the impact of a cyber attack. It also helps responders develop effective strategies for making swift strategic and operational decisions in the face of a threat.[101]

In addition to developing effective strategies, cyber incident response training also helps responders understand the scope of cyber threats and possess the necessary knowledge to respond quickly and effectively. Cyber incident response training can help responders identify the signs of a cyber attack, understand the tools and techniques used by attackers, and develop the skills needed to contain and mitigate the impact of an attack. Furthermore, training can help responders understand organisational and operational priorities, identify areas for improvement or additional investment, and develop relationships between organisations and individuals to collaborate during an actual incident.

Training of incident responders can take many forms, including a broad range of tertiary and vocational offerings, offered by a wide range of public and private training providers.

One of the most common ways cyber criminals get access to your data is through employees. For example, phishing, where fraudulent emails impersonating a person or organisation may ask for personal details or for access to certain files. Links often seem legitimate to an untrained eye and it's easy to fall into the trap. This is why employee awareness is vital. One of the most efficient ways to protect against cyber attacks is to train employees on cyber prevention and educate them of current cyber attack tools and techniques.

Research[102] into the psychology of cyber security education programs revealed the need to recognise cyber security is not solely a technical discipline but also a field deeply influenced by human factors (as discussed earlier). The research seeks to enrich cyber security education by infusing psychological insights into the curriculum, enabling students to better understand and address the psychological aspects of cyber threats and defences.

The study highlights that cyber security incidents often involve human factors, such as social engineering, cognitive biases, and user behaviour. Understanding these psychological elements is fundamental for effective cyber defence. The authors emphasise that while technical skills are crucial, they should be complemented by psychological knowledge to address the evolving landscape of cyber threats.

A pedagogical approach that incorporates psychological principles into cyber security education which goes beyond technical skills and encourages students to explore the human dimensions of cyber security is needed. The integration of psychology involves the examination of topics like cyber risk perception, decision-making biases, user training, and the psychology of cybercriminals.

Further, an interdisciplinary learning approach by fostering collaboration between psychology and cyber security disciplines is required. It encourages educators to draw from psychological theories and research to inform cyber security instruction. Such an interdisciplinary approach equips students with a well-rounded understanding of cyber security that encompasses both technical and human elements.

This should have practical implications for cyber security educators, curriculum developers, and institutions. It underscores the importance of designing curricula that address the psychological aspects of cyber threats. Educators are encouraged to incorporate case studies, simulations, and experiential learning exercises that expose students to real-world scenarios where psychology plays a central role. Employees equipped with a deep understanding of human behaviour in the context of cyber security are better prepared to mitigate threats and address vulnerabilities effectively.

Research[103] into cyber security awareness campaigns and why so many of them fail to change behaviour addresses the persistent challenge of changing user behaviour in the realm of cyber security. Despite the proliferation of cyber security awareness campaigns, cyber threats continue to exploit human vulnerabilities.

The authors recognise the importance of understanding why these campaigns often fail to produce lasting changes in user behaviour by adopting a behavioural economics perspective, offering a fresh approach to examining cyber security awareness and behaviour change. They explore the cognitive biases and heuristics that influence decision-making in the context of cyber security, emphasising that individuals often deviate from rational security practices due to cognitive biases like over-optimism, present bias, and the availability heuristic.

This research underscores that awareness campaigns alone may not be sufficient to drive behavioural change. While these campaigns can improve knowledge, they often neglect the cognitive biases and psychological factors that affect decision-making. Awareness campaigns tend to rely on the assumption that increasing knowledge will automatically lead to more secure behaviours. The research challenges this assumption, highlighting the need to address cognitive biases and heuristics.

Traditional awareness campaigns often employ fear-based messaging – particularly ones which require end user retraining if they consistently do the wrong thing – which may not effectively motivate behaviour change in the long term, such campaigns can lead to desensitisation and fatalism among users.

Educators should consider behavioural change strategies grounded in behavioural economics, such as nudging and choice architecture. These strategies leverage human biases to encourage more secure behaviours. Nudging involves designing the choice environment to guide individuals toward more secure options without restricting their freedom of choice. Choice architecture focuses on presenting security options in ways that make the desired behaviour more salient and appealing. Additionally, is the importance of tailoring interventions to specific contexts and user groups. Cyber security awareness campaigns should consider the individual's knowledge, beliefs, and biases within their unique context.

Further research[104] examines the relationship between culture and cyber security awareness. It recognises that individuals' cyber security behaviours are influenced not only by their personal characteristics but also by the culture within their organisations.

The research seeks to uncover the multifaceted dynamics at play in shaping employees' awareness and behaviours regarding information security. It places a strong emphasis on the influence of organisational culture on information security. It highlights that organisational culture encompasses shared beliefs, values, norms, and practices that impact how employees perceive and respond to security threats. The authors contend that a positive security culture can foster a proactive and security-conscious workforce, while a negative culture may result in complacency or disregard for security measures.

The research employs a survey-based approach to gather data on participants' information security awareness, as well as their perceptions of their organisation's security culture. The combination of self-reported awareness and cultural assessments provides a comprehensive view of the relationships between individual awareness and the broader cultural context.

The research finds that individuals' information security awareness is influenced by various factors, including their experience, training, and knowledge of security policies. Interestingly, the study reveals that while training and policy knowledge are significant contributors to awareness, they do not exist in isolation from the organisational culture. This underscores the interplay between individual factors and the cultural context within which security practices are embedded.

Employees' perceptions of their organisation's security culture significantly impact their information security awareness. A culture that emphasises security as a shared responsibility and encourages reporting of security incidents tends to promote greater awareness and vigilance among employees. Conversely, a culture that downplays the importance of security or lacks clear communication on security matters can hinder information security awareness efforts. Therefore, the cultural context in which security practices occur is a powerful determinant of success, particularly the mutual influence between individual factors and the broader cultural context within organisations, providing a foundation for improving cyber security awareness initiatives and practices.

Cognitive Theory, as formulated by Jean Piaget[105], focuses on how individuals acquire, process, and organise information as they develop intellectually. While Piaget's theory is primarily associated with child development, its principles can be applied to cyber security end-user awareness and training programs in the following ways:

1. Understanding Cognitive Development Stages: Piaget's theory identifies distinct cognitive development stages, such as sensorimotor, preoperational, concrete operational, and formal operational stages. In the context of cyber security training, understanding the cognitive capabilities and limitations of end-users at different stages can help tailor training materials and methods to their cognitive readiness. For instance, young children may

require simplified, visual materials, while adults may benefit from more complex explanations.

2. Assimilation and Accommodation: Piaget introduced the concepts of assimilation (fitting new information into existing mental structures) and accommodation (adapting mental structures to incorporate new information). In cyber security training, this concept can be applied by first assessing the existing knowledge and misconceptions of end-users. Training programs can then be designed to assimilate new cyber security information into their current mental models and accommodate changes when necessary.

3. Concrete vs. Abstract Thinking: Piaget's theory highlights the development of abstract thinking capabilities as individuals grow. Cyber security awareness training can adapt to these cognitive changes by gradually introducing more abstract concepts and advanced topics. Training materials should evolve to meet the cognitive abilities of end-users at various stages of development.

4. Problem-Solving Skills: Cognitive development involves the enhancement of problem-solving skills. Cyber security training can incorporate interactive scenarios and simulations that challenge end-users to apply their problem-solving abilities in realistic cyber threat situations. This can help them develop effective responses and decision-making skills.

5. Metacognition: Piaget's theory also touches on metacognition, which involves understanding one's own thought processes and the ability to think about

thinking. Cyber security training can encourage metacognitive awareness by prompting end-users to reflect on their cyber security behaviours and decision-making. This self-awareness can lead to more responsible online practices.

6. Scaffolding: Piaget's theory suggests that learners can benefit from scaffolding, where they receive guidance and support from more knowledgeable individuals. In cyber security training, mentors or educators can provide scaffolding by offering guidance and assistance to end-users, helping them bridge their cognitive gaps and acquire advanced cyber security knowledge.

Social Learning Theory, as formulated by Albert Bandura[106], emphasises the role of observational learning, modelling, and self-efficacy in shaping behaviour. These concepts can be applied to improve the safety and security of internet users in the following ways:

1. Modelling Secure Behaviour: Internet users can learn secure online behaviours by observing and modelling the actions of others. Cyber security organisations and educators can provide role models who demonstrate best practices in online safety. This might include showcasing individuals who effectively use password managers, enable multi-factor authentication, or practice safe browsing habits.

2. Self-Efficacy and Empowerment: Bandura's theory highlights the importance of self-efficacy, which refers to an individual's belief in their ability to perform a specific task. To improve internet users' online safety, training programs can focus on building

self-efficacy by providing users with practical skills and knowledge. When users feel confident in their ability to protect themselves online, they are more likely to adopt secure behaviours.

3. Observational Learning: Bandura's theory suggests that individuals can learn from observing the consequences of others' actions. Cyber security awareness campaigns can leverage this by sharing real-life examples of both the positive outcomes of secure behaviour and the negative consequences of cyber threats, such as identity theft or data breaches.

4. Peer and Community Influence: Bandura's theory recognises the influence of peers and communities in shaping behaviour. Online communities and social groups can play a significant role in promoting secure online practices. These communities can share resources, offer support, and collectively reinforce the importance of cyber security.

5. Behavioural Reinforcement: Social Learning Theory also emphasises the role of rewards and punishments in behaviour modification. Cyber security programs can incorporate positive reinforcement, such as recognition and incentives, for individuals who consistently practice secure online behaviours. Conversely, consequences for risky behaviour can serve as a deterrent.

6. Interactive and Collaborative Learning: Bandura's theory supports the idea of interactive and collaborative learning experiences. Cyber security training and awareness programs can encourage users to collaborate and share their knowledge and

experiences in secure online practices. This collaborative approach fosters a sense of community and shared responsibility for online safety.

7. Continuous Learning and Updates: Social Learning Theory acknowledges that learning is an ongoing process. Cyber security education should not be a one-time event but rather a continuous effort to keep users informed about evolving threats and best practices. Regular updates and reminders can reinforce secure behaviours over time.

Ecological Systems Theory, developed by Urie Bronfenbrenner[107], focuses on the influence of various systems in an individual's environment on their development. While this theory is primarily applied to human development, its principles can be adapted to educate internet users about online safety and security:

1. Microsystem (Immediate Environment): In Bronfenbrenner's theory, the microsystem represents an individual's immediate environment, such as family, school, and peer groups. In the context of online safety education, educators can emphasise the role of families and schools in teaching safe online practices. For example, parents can be educated on how to guide their children's internet use, and schools can incorporate cyber security lessons into the curriculum.

2. Mesosystem (Interactions Between Microsystems): The mesosystem highlights the interactions and connections between different systems within an individual's environment. Internet safety education can promote collaboration and communication

between various stakeholders, including parents, teachers, and community organisations. This can create a more cohesive and coordinated approach to educating internet users.

3. Exosystem (External Environments): Bronfenbrenner's theory includes the exosystem, which represents external environments that indirectly impact an individual, such as government policies and media influence. Internet safety campaigns can advocate for policies that promote cyber security and raise awareness of the media's role in shaping online behaviours.

4. Macrosystem (Cultural Context): The macrosystem encompasses the broader cultural context that influences an individual's development. In online safety education, recognising the cultural diversity of internet users is essential. Tailoring educational materials to reflect different cultural perspectives on cyber security can enhance relevance and effectiveness.

5. Chronosystem (Time and Development): Bronfenbrenner's theory acknowledges the role of time and life events in shaping development. Internet safety education should consider the evolving nature of cyber threats and adapt content to address current challenges. Additionally, it should cater to users of different ages and levels of digital literacy.

6. Environmental Press: Bronfenbrenner's theory introduces the concept of environmental press, which refers to the demands and challenges posed by the environment. Internet safety education can

prepare users to navigate these challenges by providing practical guidance and resources. For example, teaching users how to recognise phishing emails or secure their social media accounts.

7. Person-Environment Fit: The theory also highlights the importance of a person-environment fit. Internet safety education can help users assess their own cyber security practices and adapt them to align with their online activities and needs. This includes recognising that different online contexts may require different safety measures.

Positive psychology, pioneered by Martin Seligman[108], focuses on well-being, happiness, and the cultivation of positive emotions and strengths. While this psychological theory typically addresses individuals' mental and emotional states, its principles can be applied to encourage positive internet user behaviour and promote a safer online environment:

1. Promoting Cyber Well-Being: Emphasising mental well-being and resilience. Applied to the online world, this can involve promoting digital well-being and mental health awareness. Internet users can be encouraged to practice mindfulness, manage screen time, and engage in positive online experiences to maintain their well-being.

2. Online Positivity and Kindness: Encouraging acts of kindness and positive interactions. Efforts can be made to create a culture of positivity and kindness online. Campaigns and initiatives can promote respectful and empathetic communication, reducing online harassment and cyber bullying.

3. Digital Flourishing: Just as positive psychology seeks to help individuals flourish in life, online platforms and services can be designed to foster digital flourishing. This involves creating online spaces where users can develop their skills, pursue their interests, and experience a sense of accomplishment.

4. Digital Resilience: Highlight the importance of resilience in facing life's challenges. In the digital realm, promoting digital resilience can involve providing users with the tools and knowledge to protect themselves from cyber threats, such as phishing scams and identity theft.

5. Positive Feedback Loops: Platforms and apps can incorporate positive feedback mechanisms that reward positive behaviour. For example, users who contribute positively to online communities could receive recognition or incentives to continue their positive contributions.

6. Online Support Communities: Recognise the value of social support. Online platforms can facilitate the creation of supportive communities where users can seek help and advice, particularly when dealing with online harassment or cyberbullying.

7. Online Skill Development: Encourage the cultivation of strengths and skills. Online education and training programs can incorporate this concept by helping users develop digital literacy skills and online safety practices.

8. Digital Detox and Balance: Support balance in life. Promote a healthy balance between online and

offline activities can reduce the negative impacts of excessive screen time and digital addiction.

9. Positive User Experiences: Online platforms and applications can prioritise creating positive user experiences by designing user interfaces that are intuitive, enjoyable, and user-friendly.

10. Online Positive Feedback: Encouraging and recognising positive behaviour online can create a positive feedback loop, motivating users to continue behaving in constructive and ethical ways.

Exercises

A cyber security exercise is a simulated event that tests the readiness of an organisation to respond to a cyber attack. It is a proactive approach to identify vulnerabilities in the organisation's security infrastructure and to test the effectiveness of the incident response plan.

There are different types of cyber security exercises, such as tabletop exercises, functional exercises, and full-scale exercises. Tabletop exercises are discussion-based exercises that simulate a cyber attack scenario and test the organisation's response plan. Functional exercises are more complex than tabletop exercises and involve the deployment of resources to simulate a cyber attack scenario. Full-scale exercises are the most comprehensive type of cyber security exercise and involve the deployment of resources and personnel to simulate a real-world cyber incident scenario.

Specifically, conducting cyber security incident exercises can provide several benefits to organisations, including:

1. Test the effectiveness of their incident response plan (IRP) by simulating a cyber attack which may identify any gaps or areas for improvement.

2. Train incident response teams (IRTs) to recognise, handle and respond to cyber security incidents. Conducting exercises can help IRTs to build muscle memory and improve their readiness to combat a data breach or cyber attack.

3. Reduce the impact of a cyber incident by learning to detect and contain cyber threats and restore affected systems faster, potentially reducing lost revenue, regulatory fines and other costs associated with these threats.

4. Improve communication: The IRP contains communication information and defines the metrics associated with the incident response capability. Conducting exercises can help organizations to review their communication requirements and identify the participants in incident communication.

5. Review cyber security threats and attack vectors: Organisations should review cyber security threats and attack vectors to understand the importance of the IRP and review response activities.

6. Manage reporting and conduct IRP maintenance: The IRP provides a road map for implementing the incident response capability as defined by the organisation's mission, size, structure, functions, strategies and goals.

Research[109] into cyber defence exercises explores a multidimensional approach that recognising cyber security is not solely a technical domain, but one deeply impacted by emotional, social, and cognitive factors. The research seeks to advance the understanding of how cyber defence exercises can be designed to simulate real-world scenarios and engage participants in addressing not only technical but also human-centric challenges.

The study emphasises the importance of emotional intelligence in cyber security, particularly in high-pressure situations such as cyber attacks. It underscores that participants' emotional responses can significantly impact their decision-making and problem-solving abilities. It explores ways to incorporate emotional dimensions into cyber defence exercises, fostering emotional resilience and adaptive responses to cyber threats.

The research delves into the social aspects of cyber defence, recognising that teamwork, communication, and collaboration are critical in responding effectively to cyber incidents. It discusses the design of exercises that encourage participants to work together, simulate interpersonal challenges, and build social skills necessary for coordinated cyber defence.

Further, it acknowledges the cognitive demands placed on cyber defenders, including the need for rapid problem-solving, critical thinking, and decision-making. It explores methods for integrating cognitive challenges into exercises, such as complex scenarios that require participants to analyse information, prioritise actions, and adapt strategies in real time.

The findings have practical implications for cyber defence exercise designers and organisations. They highlight the need to move beyond technical simulations and consider the holistic development of cyber defence competencies.

By emphasising that a multidimensional approach to cyber defence exercises contributes to the development of cyber resilience among participants, along with addressing emotional, social, and cognitive aspects, cyber response exercises better prepare individuals and teams to navigate the dynamic and challenging landscape of cyber security.

There are several models available for simulating cyber incident response. One such model is the NIST Special Publication (SP) 800-61. This publication provides guidelines and recommendations for establishing, managing, and improving computer security incident response capabilities within an organisation.

The goal of SP 800-61 is to help organisations effectively prepare for, respond to, and recover from computer security incidents. It outlines a systematic approach to incident handling, covering various aspects such as incident detection, analysis, containment, eradication, recovery, and post-incident activities. The document emphasizes the importance of creating an incident response capability that is well-integrated into an organization's overall cybersecurity program.

SP 800-61 is a valuable resource for security professionals, incident responders, and organisations seeking to enhance their ability to manage and mitigate the impact of cyber security incidents. It provides a framework for creating an incident response plan, establishing communication protocols, and fostering coordination among different teams within an organisation to respond promptly and effectively to security incidents.[110]

Cyber security is also full of 'colours' with respect to incident response. One significant one is 'purple'. A purple team exercise is a cyber security assessment methodology that combines elements of both red teaming and blue teaming. The purpose of a purple team exercise is to improve an organisation's overall cyber security posture by fostering collaboration and communication between offensive (red team) and defensive (blue team) security teams.

In a traditional red teaming scenario, a team simulates cyber adversaries to identify vulnerabilities and weaknesses in the organisation's security defences. On the other hand, the blue team focuses on defence and response, working to detect and mitigate potential threats.

In a purple team exercise, these two teams collaborate closely. The red team provides simulated attacks, and the blue team responds to these simulations in real-time. The collaboration allows for a more dynamic and interactive assessment of the organisation's security capabilities. The purple team approach encourages knowledge sharing, feedback, and mutual learning between the offensive and defensive teams. This helps organisations not only identify vulnerabilities but also improve their incident detection and response capabilities.

A purple team exercise is an effective way for organisations to validate and enhance their cyber security measures by combining the strengths of both offensive and defensive security teams in a collaborative and educational environment.

When asked "How satisfied are you with the incident response training and exercises provided by your organisation?", 37% of respondents said 'moderately satisfied', followed by 25% being 'neither satisfied nor dissatisfied'. Considering 11% of respondents were 'extremely dissatisfied', I think there is a fair way to go to improve the incident response training and exercising by organisations.

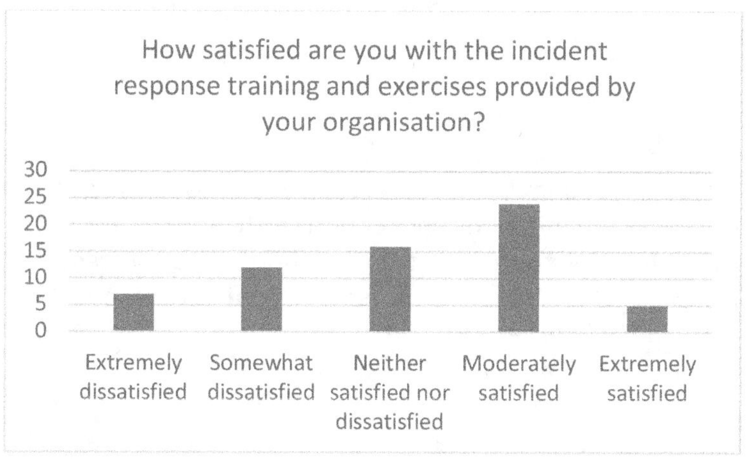

Following on from these figures, when asked "How well-prepared do you feel your organisation is to handle emerging cyber threats and attacks?", over half (54%) of respondents thought 'very well' and 'moderately well'. Whilst there is outlying statistics at either end, broadly speaking I think this is quite a positive response.

Added to the above analysis, when asked "How frequently does your organisation conduct post-incident reviews to assess the effectiveness of the incident response process?", pleasingly 30% of respondents stated 'regularly', followed by 28% stating 'after every incident'.

Overall, there seems to be a general satisfaction with incident response training and exercising, combined with a feeling of general preparedness for responding to a cyber incident. However the low levels of post-incident review is concerning.

The Role of Threat Intelligence

Cyber threat intelligence (CTI) is a critical component of modern cyber security. It refers to the knowledge and insights gained from collecting, analysing, and interpreting data related to potential cyber threats and vulnerabilities. This intelligence helps organisations understand the evolving threat landscape, including the tactics, techniques, and procedures employed by cyber adversaries.

Cyber threat intelligence provides actionable information that enables organisations to proactively identify and mitigate cyber risks, fortify their defences, and respond effectively to security incidents. It empowers cyber security teams with the contextual understanding needed to make informed decisions, enhancing an organisation's overall security posture in an ever-changing digital environment.

The information gained from a competent threat intelligence program can enhance the incident response process. Predicting a cyber-attack with precision is challenging, but threat intelligence can significantly enhance an organisation's ability to anticipate and prepare for potential threats. Organisations my use threat intelligence by:

1. Providing early warning indicators such as unusual network activity, known attack patterns, and vulnerabilities that threat actors may exploit.

2. Enabling organisations to analyse historical attack trends and patterns.

3. Creating attributes and profiles about threat actor groups, their motivations, and their targets.

4. Monitoring publicly available information on the internet to gather intelligence about potential threats.

5. Analysing user behaviour to detect anomalies in user and network behaviour.

6. Sharing of Indicators of Compromise (IoC), such as malicious IP addresses, file hashes, or malware signatures, with industry-specific Information Sharing and Analysis Centres (ISACs) or other threat intelligence-sharing communities.

7. Integration with machine learning and artificial intelligence algorithms to identify patterns and anomalies in vast datasets.

8. Conduct of red team exercises that simulate cyber attacks using threat intelligence.

It's important to note that while threat intelligence can significantly improve an organisation's predictive capabilities, it's not a foolproof method. Threat landscapes are dynamic, and threat actors continuously adapt their tactics. Therefore, organisations should complement threat intelligence with robust cyber security practices, proactive defence measures, and incident response planning to effectively mitigate cyber threats.

Threat intelligence can not only be used to predict a cyber attack, but it also plays a crucial role for organisations to respond to a cyber attack effectively. This may include:

1. When an incident is detected, threat intelligence may help incident responders prioritise and triage the incident. It can provide information about the severity, attribution, and potential impact of the

attack, enabling responders to allocate resources effectively.

2. Providing information about threat actor groups, their tactics, techniques, and motivations. This attribution can help organisations understand the context of the attack and determine whether it aligns with known threat actor behaviour.

3. Providing context around the attack, including the attacker's methods and goals. This contextual information assists responders in understanding the attack's scope and potential objectives.

4. Enriching incident data with additional context, such as known attack infrastructure or tactics. This enrichment aids in the investigation process by providing additional leads to follow and indicators to monitor.

5. Creating custom signatures and rules for their security tools, such as intrusion detection systems and security information and event management systems. These custom rules can trigger alerts when matching IoCs are detected.

6. Anticipating attacker behaviour and tactics, providing information to develop response playbooks and decision trees for various attack scenarios.

7. Contributing back to the threat intelligence community by sharing newly discovered IoCs and attack patterns. This collaborative approach helps the community at large respond more effectively to similar threats.

8. Adapting defences in real-time. When new intelligence is received, organisations can adjust their security controls, update firewall rules, and implement blocking or containment measures.

The future of cyber threat intelligence in incident response holds several key developments:

1. Automation and Orchestration: Incident response may increasingly rely on automation and orchestration to streamline processes. Machine learning and AI can be used to analyse threat intelligence data and automate response actions, allowing for rapid and consistent reactions to emerging threats.

2. Enhanced Threat Detection: Cyber threat intelligence may become more granular and sophisticated, enabling organisations to detect subtle and advanced threats. This will involve the integration of threat intelligence with security analytics, machine learning, and behavioural analysis to identify anomalous behaviour and potential threats.

3. Contextualisation: The future of threat intelligence should emphasise the importance of context. Threat indicators will be analysed in the context of an organisation's specific environment, including its assets, vulnerabilities, and industry sector. This contextualisation will enable more accurate threat prioritisation and response.

4. Threat Sharing and Collaboration: Threat intelligence sharing among organisations and sectors needs to continue to grow. Public and private sector collaboration will expand, fostering the exchange of

actionable threat information. This collective defence approach will enhance incident response capabilities across the board.

5. Deeper Understanding of Threat Actors: Cyber threat intelligence will focus on gaining a deeper understanding of threat actors, their motivations, and their tactics, techniques, and procedures (TTPs). This knowledge will inform proactive threat hunting and the development of tailored response strategies.

6. Integration with Cloud Security: As organisations move more of their operations to the cloud, threat intelligence needs to integrate with cloud security platforms. This integration will enable real-time threat detection and response across hybrid and multi-cloud environments.

7. Zero Trust Framework: The adoption of a zero trust security model should drive the need for continuous monitoring and threat intelligence. Organisations should apply threat intelligence to enforce access controls and detect anomalous behaviour within their networks.

8. Geopolitical and Geostrategic Threat Intelligence: Understanding geopolitical and geostrategic factors will become crucial for organisations with international interests. Threat intelligence should encompass geopolitical insights to anticipate state-sponsored threats and their potential impact.

9. Privacy and Ethical Considerations: The collection and sharing of threat intelligence will be subject to increased scrutiny in terms of privacy and ethical concerns. Organisations will need to navigate these

issues while harnessing the benefits of threat intelligence.

10. Skill Development: As the complexity of cyber threats and the volume of threat data grow, there will be an increased demand for skilled professionals in threat intelligence analysis and incident response. Organisations need to invest in training and workforce development to meet this demand.

Research[111], focusing on the energy sector – particularly relevant given the increasing digitalisation of critical infrastructure and the potential vulnerabilities it introduces – has focused on the development of a CTI Framework tailored to incident response within the Energy Cloud Platform. This framework acknowledges the unique challenges faced by the energy sector in terms of security and resilience.

The CTI Framework combines elements of proactive threat intelligence, incident detection, and response coordination, providing a comprehensive approach to cyber security in the energy sector. It also incorporates real-time data collection, threat analysis, and integration with incident response procedures, offering a holistic view of the cyber threat landscape.

Underscoring the critical importance of incident response within the Energy Cloud Platform, where disruptions can have severe consequences on energy production, distribution, and reliability, the authors emphasised the need for rapid and informed incident response, facilitated by the CTI Framework's capabilities in identifying and assessing threats in real-time. Incident response procedures are detailed, highlighting the integration of threat intelligence into the decision-making process, which is crucial for minimising the impact of cyber incidents.

A key finding of this research is the effectiveness of integrating threat intelligence into incident response. The CTI Framework facilitates the timely identification of threats, enabling proactive measures to mitigate risks. It also highlighted the role of machine learning and AI in automating threat analysis, which is particularly valuable given the large volume of data generated in the Energy Cloud Platform.

The research did however acknowledge the challenges of implementing the CTI Framework in practice, including the need for data sharing and collaboration among energy stakeholders and the need to integrate threat intelligence into critical incident response decision-making processes.

The Role of Government Agencies

When a cyber attack occurs, coordination between government agencies and the victim organisation is crucial to minimise the current damage and prevent future attacks. Government agencies directly or indirectly linked to the affected organisations should have clarity around their internal roles and responsibilities. This includes knowing when and how to escalate the issue to other departments, such as police; when and how to alert the private sector and public; and what information to release to media.

Cyber security exercises are a vital element for planning, preparing, and responding to cyber security incidents. They enable government and industry to test plans and processes, understand organisational and operational priorities, identify areas for improvement or additional investment, and develop relationships between organisations and individuals to collaborate during an actual incident. This should dovetail with various national cyber security strategies, including a dedicated national cyber security agency, a national critical infrastructure protection program, a national incident response and recovery plan, defined laws pertaining to all cybercrimes, and a vibrant cyber security ecosystem.[112]

There are many government agencies which play various roles during a cyber incident. This includes various law enforcement agencies, including police and regulators (including those responsible for civil penalties resulting from a data breach) and various national security agencies, including those who collect signals intelligence or administer critical infrastructure protection schemes. They can all assist in various:

1. Investigation: Police are responsible for investigating cybercrimes. They collect and analyse evidence to identify perpetrators and occasionally prosecute offenders. They understand the legal aspects of cybercrimes, ensuring incident response is conducted within the boundaries of the law.

2. Coordination: Law enforcement agencies have traditionally been a central point of contact, coordinating efforts between various organisations involved in incident response, such as government agencies, private sector entities, and international partners. However, this is changing as some governments create a central a government CERT or a standalone agency for the protection of critical infrastructure.

3. Threat Intelligence Sharing: Signals intelligence agencies have access to extensive databases and threat intelligence. They can share information about cyber threats and attack patterns, enabling organisations to strengthen their defences and prevent future incidents.

4. Victim Support: Police provide support to cybercrime victims. This support can include guidance on mitigating damages, legal assistance, and counselling services for individuals or organisations affected by the incident.

5. International Cooperation: Police can facilitate cooperation between countries in investigating cross-border cyber incidents. This collaboration is essential due to the international nature of most serious and organised cybercrimes.

6. Public Awareness and Education: Law enforcement agencies have also traditionally raised public awareness about cyber threats and best practices for cyber security, just like they do for most crime types. However, this is also changing in some jurisdictions with the creation of dedicated e-safety offices dedicated to helping individuals and organisations understand risks, and thereby reducing the likelihood of falling victim to cybercrimes.

7. Policy Development: Government agencies, more broadly, contribute to the development of cyber security policies and regulations. They provide insights based on their experience in dealing with cybercrimes, assisting parliament in creating effective legislation to combat cyber threats.

When analysing the above points, it is the police which play the most important role. The question arising out of this, is how many times has there been incident response exercising between private sector organisations and national law enforcement agencies?

Law enforcement, particularly policing agencies play a critical role in the ecosystem of combatting cybercrime. For too long policing agencies have used jurisdictional issues as an excuse to not commence an investigation.

The Role of CSIRTs

A CSIRT (Computer Security Incident Response Team) is a service, usually within an organisation (but may also be external) that is responsible for receiving, reviewing and responding to computer security incident reports and activity. The purpose of the CSIRT is to develop and promote best management practices and technology applications to resist attacks on networked systems, to limit damage, and to ensure continuity of critical services. CSIRTs provide a range of services including proactive and reactive services, as well as security quality management functions.[113]

The first CERT (Computer Emergency Response Team) was formed by the United States Department of Defence and Carnegie Mellon University in 1988. It was created to improve communication, avoid redundant analysis, and ensure timely defensive and corrective measures to limit the damage done by cyber incidents. Since this time there has been the creation of CSIRTs for industry sectors, vendors, consultancies, and organisations.[114]

Information sharing between CSIRTs during (and after) a cyber security incident would seem a logical and important function. Though there may be some impediments to this, including jurisdictional and legal issues (with the sharing of sensitive data across borders), along with deficiencies in trust, which may be exacerbated by commercial drivers.

CSIRTs serve as a crucial line of defence against cyber threats, and their performance directly impacts an organisation's security posture. Research findings from a combination of survey data and interviews, allowing for a comprehensive assessment of CSIRT operations and effectiveness, revealing

CSIRTs vary in their effectiveness, which can be attributed to factors such as team structure, communication protocols, and the level of training and expertise among team members. Unsurprisingly, CSIRTs with well-defined roles, clear communication channels, and members who receive ongoing training tend to exhibit higher levels of effectiveness.[115]

CSIRT team structures and dynamics in determining their effectiveness. Team cohesion, leadership, and collaboration play pivotal roles. Effective CSIRTs often possess well-defined roles and responsibilities for team members, ensuring that everyone knows their specific duties during an incident. The presence of strong leadership and decision-making processes is crucial in responding promptly and effectively to cyber incidents. Effective CSIRTs often maintain a balance between centralised coordination and decentralised autonomy, allowing for flexibility and adaptability in response.[116]

Communication is identified as a critical factor influencing CSIRT effectiveness. Timely and effective communication within the team and with external stakeholders is imperative. CSIRTs that establish clear communication protocols, including incident reporting mechanisms and escalation procedures, are better equipped to respond efficiently. Regular communication with other organisational units, such as IT and legal departments, enhances incident coordination and resolution. Findings emphasise the importance of continuous training in communication skills to ensure that CSIRT members can effectively convey complex technical information to non-technical stakeholders.[117]

The research underscores the role of training and skill development in CSIRT effectiveness. Continuous learning and skill enhancement are essential in the rapidly evolving cyber security landscape. Effective CSIRTs prioritise ongoing training for their members, keeping them up-to-date with the latest threats and incident response techniques. Cross-training and knowledge sharing within the team contribute to a versatile skill set among CSIRT members, enabling them to tackle diverse challenges. Collaboration with external organisations, such as industry groups and information sharing communities, is also identified as a valuable source of knowledge and skill development.

Organisations should invest in their CSIRTs by cultivating an environment that promotes continuous learning, clear communication, and effective incident response practices. This research serves as a valuable resource for organisations seeking to optimise their cyber security incident response capabilities in an ever-evolving threat landscape.

When asked "When responding to a cyber security incident, how important is it for you to have clear roles and responsibilities defined within the incident response team?", 55% of survey respondents stated 'extremely important', followed by 33% stating 'important'.

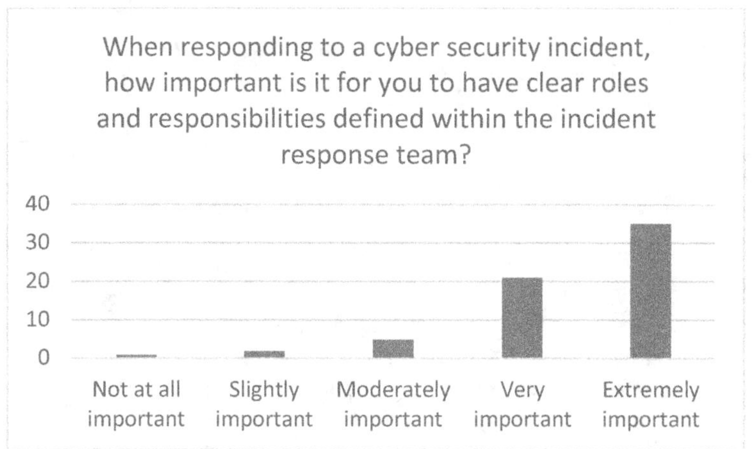

When survey recipients were asked "How often do you encounter unexpected challenges or obstacles during the incident response process?", 52% stated 'most of the time, followed by 25% stating 'always'. Combining these results highlights the need for defined roles to tackle unexpected challenges which occur during incident response.

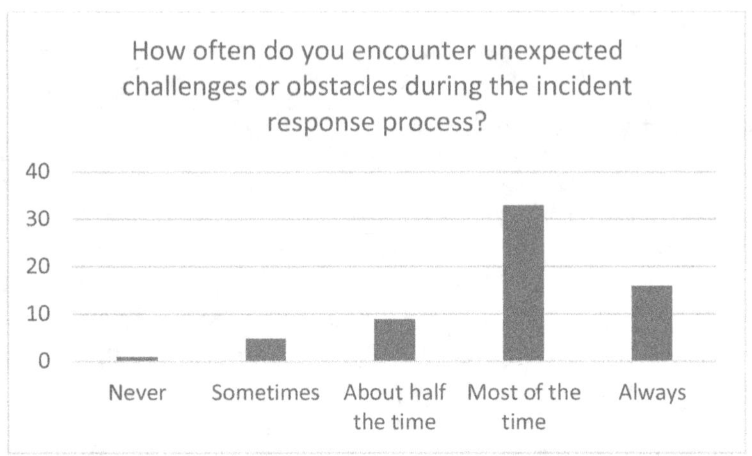

Additional research of CSIRTs from an organisational psychology perspective, offers a unique lens to understand the dynamics and effectiveness of these teams. Examining team cohesion, communication, leadership, motivation, and stress, it emerged team cohesion is a critical factor, with findings suggesting that highly cohesive CSIRTs are better equipped to respond effectively to incidents. Effective communication within CSIRTs and with external stakeholders is pivotal. The study highlights the role of communication in information sharing, decision-making, and incident resolution.[118]

Leadership qualities and styles significantly impact CSIRT performance, with effective leaders fostering a culture of trust and collaboration within the team. This helped motivation, both intrinsic and extrinsic, as a driver for CSIRT members' commitment and performance. Stress and burnout are acknowledged as prevalent issues among CSIRT members, taking a psychological toll from incident response and recognising the importance of stress management strategies.[119]

The significance of team composition, emphasising the value of diverse skill sets and expertise within CSIRTs, is seen as a critical aspect of success. Further, training and development programs play a pivotal role in enhancing CSIRT capabilities.[120]

When survey respondents were asked "How would you rate the level of collaboration and communication between your organisation and internal stakeholders during a cyber security incident?", 42% responded with 'average', followed by 34% stating 'good'.

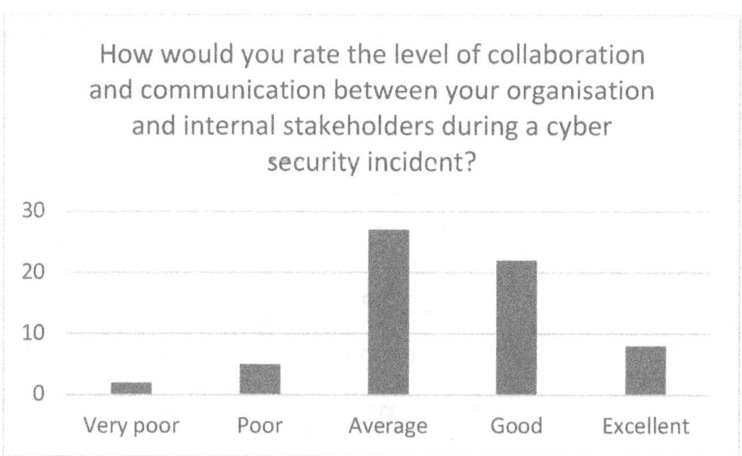

Understanding the psychological and communication dynamics of CSIRTs is crucial for optimising team performance. It highlights the comprehensive exploration of psychological factors affecting CSIRTs, the interdisciplinary approach adopted by some organisations, and the practical implications of their findings for the cyber security community.

Organisational Governance

Governance refers to the framework of rules, processes, and structures through which decisions are made and authority is exercised. It encompasses the mechanisms that ensure accountability, transparency, and alignment with the organisation's goals and values.

Governance plays a role in aligning cyber security efforts with organisational objectives, ensuring adequate resource allocation, and fostering a culture of security. From a practical standpoint, recognising the importance of governance in cyber security, many organisations have sought frameworks and models to guide their governance strategies.[121]

In the context of cyber incident response, governance extends to the establishment of policies, procedures, and structures that guide how the organisation detects, responds to, and recovers from cyber threats. It involves defining roles and responsibilities, ensuring compliance with relevant regulations, and creating a framework for communication and decision-making during a security incident. An effective governance structure in cyber security is crucial for orchestrating a coordinated and efficient response to mitigate the impact of incidents and safeguard the organisation's digital assets.

An incident response structure should dovetail into an organisations' overarching governance framework, detailing the approach to handling and mitigating cyber security incidents. This includes:

- Development of clear policies outlining the roles, responsibilities, and escalation procedures within the incident response team.
- Compliance with relevant legal and regulatory requirements, along with adherence to industry standards and best practices.
- Defined leadership roles ensuring effective decision-making.
- Establishment of communication protocols for seamless information sharing, both within the incident response team and with external stakeholders.
- Coordination with external entities, resource allocation, and documentation of incidents and responses.

When most people think of governance, they consider the role of company directors. Company directors play a crucial role by providing strategic direction and oversight, ensuring that the company operates ethically, complies with laws and regulations, and manages risks effectively. They establish policies, monitor performance, and safeguard the interests of stakeholders, contributing to the long-term sustainability and success of the organisation.

In Australia, Company directors have been put on notice by the Australian Security and Investments Commission (ASIC) that they will come under scrutiny if their businesses are hacked by cyber criminals and they failed to prioritise cyber security. The ASIC Chair stated "Cyber should always have been a top risk facing corporate Australia, it's just that recent events have reminded people why it should be considered a top risk" and further stated "For all boards, I think cyber resilience has got to be a No. 1 risk facing everyone."[122]

Since a cyber event can be devastating to an organisation, including share trading halts, loss of consumer confidence, regulatory scrutiny, and often extremely expensive, company directors should be actively considering how to mitigate the financial impact of such incidents to protect data subjects and their shareholders.

The aftermath of a successful cyber attack can be emotionally draining, leaving people feeling embarrassed, ashamed, and violated. Since cyber attacks can have a tremendous negative psychological impact, the effects of which victims can feel for weeks and months, company directors should be concerned with the mental effects of staff and as such ensure management take steps to mitigate the psychological impact of responding to cyber attacks on their staff.[123]

When asked "Does your Board of Directors recognise you might suffer negative psychological effects as a result of participating in incident response activities?" 42% of respondents stated 'no', followed by 38% saying 'Don't know'. Company directors need to reflect on these figures and whilst it is not their role to be involved in management roles or responsibilities, they need to be cognizant of the psychological issues surrounding incident response and telegraph this via board decisions.

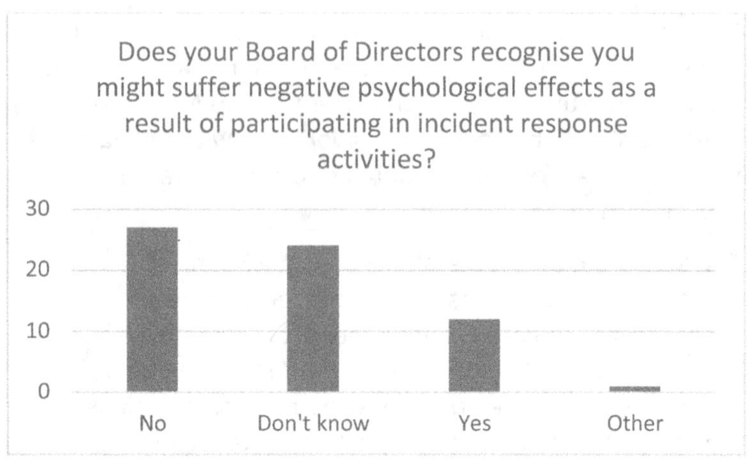

Company director cyber education has become a hot topic in recent years, featuring in numerous governance conferences and being developed by many training providers.

Key points for company directors:

1. Understanding cyber risks: Company directors should have a solid understanding of the cyber security risks facing their organisation. This includes awareness of the types of cyber threats, potential impact on business operations, and the importance of protecting sensitive data.

2. Cyber security governance: Establishing robust cyber security governance is essential. Company directors should ensure that there are clear policies, procedures, and responsibilities in place for managing cyber security risks, and that these are integrated into the overall corporate governance framework.

3. Risk management and assessment: Regularly assess and update the organisation's cyber security risk management strategy. Company directors should be informed about the current threat landscape and the effectiveness of existing cyber security measures.

4. Incident response plan: Ensure the organisation has a well-documented and tested incident response plan. This plan should outline the steps to be taken in the event of a cyber incident, including communication protocols, roles and responsibilities, and strategies for containment and recovery.

5. Board cyber security training: Company directors should undergo cyber security training to enhance their understanding of cyber threats, the importance of cyber security measures, and their role in incident response. This knowledge is vital for effective decision-making.

6. Resource allocation: Allocate sufficient resources, both financial and human, to cyber security efforts. Company directors should be aware of decisions related to cyber security budgets, ensuring that investments align with the organisation's risk profile and overall business strategy.

7. Third-party risk management: Evaluate and manage cyber security risks associated with third-party vendors and partners. Company directors should ensure that contracts and agreements with third parties include cyber security provisions and standards.

8. Insurance coverage: Assess the need for cyber security insurance and work with risk management professionals to ensure that the organisation has appropriate coverage. Company directors should be aware of policy terms and conditions.

9. Regular reporting and updates: Receive regular reports (particularly via the risk & audit committee) on the organisation's cyber security posture, incidents, and response activities. Company directors should be kept informed to make well-informed decisions and provide strategic guidance.

10. Legal and regulatory compliance: Stay informed about cyber security laws and regulations applicable to the industry and geographic locations in which the organisation operates. Ensure the organisation is compliant with relevant cyber security requirements.

11. Communication and Transparency: Foster a culture of open communication and transparency regarding cyber security matters. Company directors should encourage reporting of potential incidents and ensure that communication channels are well-defined in the incident response plan.

12. Continuous improvement: Promote a culture of continuous improvement in cyber security. Company directors should be proactive in seeking updates on emerging threats, technological advancements, and best practices to keep the organisation's cyber security measures up-to-date.

Cyber Insurance

Cyber insurance is a type of insurance coverage designed to protect individuals, businesses, and organisations from financial losses and liabilities resulting from cyber-related incidents and attacks. As the frequency and severity of cyber threats increase, cyber insurance has become an important component of risk management strategies.

Cyber insurance policies typically provide coverage for a range of potential risks associated with cyber security incidents and depending upon the policy, may include:

1. Data breaches: Coverage for the costs associated with a data breach, such as notification expenses, credit monitoring services for affected individuals, and costs related to public relations efforts.

2. Business interruption: Compensation for financial losses resulting from a disruption in business operations due to a cyber attack, malware infection, or other cyber incidents.

3. Ransomware attacks: Coverage for expenses related to ransom payments or the costs of recovering from a ransomware attack.

4. Network and system damage: Compensation for the costs of repairing or replacing damaged computer systems and networks due to a cyber incident.

5. Liability protection: Coverage for legal expenses and liabilities arising from third-party claims related to a cyber security incident, such as lawsuits from customers or business partners.

6. Regulatory fines and penalties: Coverage for fines and penalties imposed by regulatory bodies in the event of a data breach or failure to comply with cyber security regulations.

7. Crisis management: Financial support for hiring public relations and crisis management services to mitigate reputational damage following a cyber incident.

Cyber insurance policies can vary widely in terms of coverage, exclusions, and conditions. The specifics of a policy will depend on factors such as the type and size of the organisation, the industry it operates in, and the perceived level of cyber risk.

Before purchasing cyber insurance, organisations should conduct a thorough risk assessment, implement robust cyber security measures, and understand the terms and conditions of the insurance policy. Additionally, insurers may require organisations to meet certain cyber security standards and practices to qualify for coverage and to receive lower premiums. Cyber insurance is just one component of a comprehensive cybersecurity strategy, and it should be integrated with other risk management measures to enhance overall cyber resilience.

Whilst premiums increased by 10-15% on average in the first half of 2023, this increase is still lower than in previous years. The cyber insurance market has become more competitive due to sustainable loss ratios, selective underwriting, and new entrants.[124]

Cyber insurance provides a degree of financial protection to organisations in the event of a cyber-related incident, covering costs associated with data breaches, ransomware attacks, and other cyber security threats. The ability of a company to effectively demonstrate the reasons for procuring a cyber insurance policy – or not – as part of their wider cyber risk management strategy, is of critical importance.[125]

Conclusion

Empowering cyber security incident responders is critical if society is to gain the most out of our technology adoption. We need to equip individuals and organisations with the knowledge, tools, and mindset necessary to effectively navigate the dynamic landscape of cyber threats. The book emphasizes the critical role of incident responders as the first line of defence against cyber attacks, recognising them as the unsung heroes who safeguard digital assets and ensure the resilience of our interconnected world.

The central theme of empowerment permeates the book, highlighting the need for continuous learning and skill development among incident responders. Through the survey of cyber security professionals, real-world case studies and practical insights this book fosters a culture of proactivity and readiness. It emphasizes the importance of proactive incident response planning, simulation exercises, and collaboration between security teams to hone the collective capabilities of an organisation.

Furthermore, the book champions the idea that empowerment in the realm of cyber security is not just about technical proficiency; it encompasses a holistic approach that considers the psychological and emotional well-being of incident responders. It delves into the stress and pressure faced by these professionals, offering strategies for resilience, mental agility, and effective communication during high-pressure situations.

By demystifying complex cyber security concepts, promoting a continuous improvement mindset, and advocating for a human-centric approach, the book sets a foundation for transforming incident responders into proactive and empowered defenders of digital landscapes. Ultimately it serves as a beacon, guiding its readers towards a future where cyber security professionals are not just reactive responders but proactive guardians, ready to face the evolving challenges of the digital age with resilience, courage, and unwavering expertise.

1 ABS. *Cyber security incidents double between 2019-20 and 2021-22*. [https://www.abs.gov.au/media-centre/media-releases/cyber-security-incidents-double-between-2019-20-and-2021-22]

2 ASD. *Australian Signals Directorate releases 2023 ASD Cyber Threat Report*. [https://www.cyber.gov.au/about-us/view-all-content/news-and-media/2023-ASD-cyber-threat-report]

3 Ivanti. *Ivanti Insights Episode 10: Ransomware: From the '80s Floppy Disk Days to Today*. [https://www.ivanti.com/blog/ivanti-insights-episode-10-ransomware-from-the-80s-floppy-disk-days-to-today]

4 Leyden, J. *Ransomware getting harder to break*. [https://www.theregister.com/2006/07/24/ransomware/]

5 Gupta, A., & Kumar, R. (2022). *Ransomware Attacks and Defence Mechanisms: A Survey*. Sustainability, 14(1), 8.

6 Mason, A. *Ransomware 2022: Facts and Statistics*. [https://www.pentestpeople.com/ransomware-2022-facts-and-statistics/]

7 Crowdstrike. *2022 Cyber Threat Report*. [https://go.crowdstrike.com/rs/281-OBQ-266/images/Report2022GTR.pdf]

8 Sscaler. *2022 ThreatLabs State of Ransomware Report*. [https://www.sscaler.com/resources/industry-reports/2022-threatlabs-ransomware-report.pdf?_gl=1*wj2vi8*_ga*MTkwODMwMjg1Mi4xNjc0ODgwMDAy*_ga_10SPJ4YJL9*MTY3NDg4MDAwMi4xLjEuMTY3NDg4MDA2MS4xLjAuMA...]

9 Braue, D. *Global Ransomware Damage Costs Predicted To Exceed $265 Billion By 2031*. [https://cyber securityventures.com/global-ransomware-damage-costs-predicted-to-reach-250-billion-usd-by-2031/]

10 Congressional Research Service. *Colonial Pipeline: The Darkside Strikes*. [https://crsreports.congress.gov/product/pdf/IN/IN11667]

11 Claoughton, D & Beilharz, N. *JBS Foods pays $14.2 million ransom to end cyber attack on its global operations*. [https://www.abc.net.au/news/rural/2021-06-10/jbs-foods-pays-14million-ransom-cyber-attack/100204240]

12 GlobalSign. *Kaseya Attack 2021 – Are Ransomware Attacks Inevitable?* [https://www.globalsign.com/en/blog/kaseya-attack-2021-are-ransomware-attacks-inevitable]

13 Greig, J. *Acer confirms second cyberattack in 2021 after ransomware incident in March*. [https://www.zdnet.com/article/acer-confirms-second-cyberattack-in-2021/]

14 Security Intelligence. *DeepLocker: How AI Can Power a Stealthy New Breed of Malware.* [https://securityintelligence.com/deeplocker-how-ai-can-power-a-stealthy-new-breed-of-malware/]

15 Alraizza, A & Algarni, A. *Ransomware Detection Using Machine Learning: A Survey.* [https://www.mdpi.com/2504-2289/7/3/143]

16 Nvidia. *NVIDIA and Booz Allen Hamilton Expand Partnership to Bring AI-Enabled Cyber security to Public and Private Sectors.* [https://nvidianews.nvidia.com/news/nvidia-and-booz-allen-hamilton-expand-partnership-to-bring-ai-enabled-cyber security-to-public-and-private-sectors]

17 Malwarebytes. *Gandcrab.* [https://www.malwarebytes.com/gandcrab]

18 Crowdstrike. *Ransomware as a service (RAAS) Explained How it works & Examples.* [https://www.crowdstrike.com/cyber security-101/ransomware/ransomware-as-a-service-raas/]

19 Kerner, S. *Colonial Pipeline hack explained: Everything you need to know.* [https://www.techtarget.com/whatis/feature/Colonial-Pipeline-hack-explained-Everything-you-need-to-know]

20 Tudor, D. *Blackbaud Ransomware Attack 101.* [https://heimdalsecurity.com/blog/blackbaud-ransomware-attack-101/]

21 Sopra Steria. *Cyberattack: updated information.* [https://www.soprasteria.com/newsroom/press-releases/details/cyberattack-updated-information]

22 Kalia, S. *Cognizant hit by 'Maze' ransomware attack.* [https://www.reuters.com/article/cognizant-tech-cyber-idINL1N2C60A8/]

23 Skulkin, O. *Incident Response Techniques for Ransomware Attacks: Understand modern ransomware attacks and build an incident response strategy to work through them,* Packt Publishing, 2022.

24 Statistica. *Number of data records exposed worldwide from 1st quarter 2020 to 1st quarter 2023.* [https://www.statista.com/statistics/1307426/number-of-data-breaches-worldwide/]

25 IBM. *Cost of a Data Breach Report 2023.* [https://www.ibm.com/reports/data-breach]

26 OAIC. *Notifiable Data Breaches Report: July to December 2022.* [https://www.oaic.gov.au/privacy/notifiable-data-breaches/notifiable-data-breaches-publications/notifiable-data-breaches-report-july-to-december-2022]

27 Sawoad, S, Hasan, R & Asad, R. *Defending against data breaches: Strategies and challenges,* Computers & Security, vol. 72, pp. 82-97, 2018.

28 Cavusoglu, T, Mishra, B & Raghunathan, S. *Preventing data breaches through threat assessment and optimal investments in cyber security*, MIS Quarterly, vol. 41, no. 4, pp. 961-983, 2017

29 Dhillon, Y. *Protecting against data breaches: A review of strategies and challenges*, International Journal of Information Management, vol. 35, no. 6, pp. 640-644, 2015.

30 Bierstaker, S & Eining, M. *Information systems control activities in the aftermath of data security breaches*, Journal of Information Systems, vol. 24, no. 2, pp. 1-24, 2010.

31 Australian Government. *ICT Security Specialists.* [https://labourmarketinsights.gov.au/occupation-profile/ict-security-specialists?occupationCode=262112]

32 Ibid

33 Grimes, G. *Ransomware Response Plan*, in Ransomware Protection Playbook , Wiley, 2022,

34 Elson, T et al, *Cost-Benefit Analysis of an Employee Assistance Program for a Geographically Dispersed Workforce in South Australia* (2020) 35(1) Journal of workplace behavioural health 37

35 Cyber security Career. *What is Cyber Security Incident Response?* [https://cyber securitycareer.org/cyber-security-incident-response/]

36 ACSC. *Preparing for and Responding to Cyber Security Incidents.* [https://www.cyber.gov.au/resources-business-and-government/governance-and-user-education/governance/preparing-and-responding-cyber-security-incidents]

37 Aurelio, H & Maestre, A. *The Empirical Study of the Factors that Influence Threat Avoidance Behaviour in Ransomware Security Incidents.* [https://nsuworks.nova.edu/cgi/viewcontent.cgi?article=2160&context=gscis_etd]

38 Wueest, B & Carman, N. *Ransomware Response: A Decision Framework for Incident Response Teams.* NIST Interagency/Internal Report (NISTIR) - 8374

39 Neprash, H, McGlave, C & Nikpay, S. *We tried to quantify how harmful hospital ransomware attacks are for patients. Here's what we found.* [https://www.statnews.com/2023/11/17/hospital-ransomware-attack-patient-deaths-study/]

40 Papastergiou, S, Haralambos, M & Kalogeraki, E. *Cyber Security Incident Handling, Warning and Response System for the European Critical Information Infrastructures (CyberSANE)* in arXiv.org (Cornell University Library, arXiv.org, 2020)

---

41 CREST. *Cyber Security Incident Response Maturity Assessment.* [https://www.crest-approved.org/buying-building-cyber-services/cyber-security-incident-response-maturity-assessment/]

42 Johansen, G. *Digital Forensics and Incident Response: Incident Response Techniques and Procedures to Respond to Modern Cyber Threats* (Packt, Second edition., 2020)

43 Amos, Z. *The State of Burnout, a growing concern in the cyber security industry.* (2023, February 27). InCyber. [https://incyber.org/en/state-burnout-growing-concern-cyber security-industry/]

44 Ibid

45 McLeod, S. *Psychodynamic Approach In Psychology.* [https://www.simplypsychology.org/psychodynamic.html#:~: text=The%20psychodynamic%20approach%20in%20psychology,in%20shap ing%20personality%20and%20behavior.]

46 Cherry, K. *An Overview of Sigmund Freud's Theories.* [https://www.verywellmind.com/freudian-theory-2795845]

47 McLeod, S. *Freud's Theory Of Personality: Id, Ego, And Superego.* [https://www.simplypsychology.org/psyche.html]

48 Nyre-Yu, M, Gutzwiller, R & Caldwell, B. *Observing Cyber Security Incident Response: Qualitative Themes From Field Research.* Proceedings of the Human Factors and Ergonomics Society Annual Meeting, vol. 63, no. 1, 2019, pp. 437-441. Sage Publications.

49 Nyre-Yu, M, et al. *Observing Cyber Security Incident Response: Qualitative Themes from Field Research.* [https://journals.sagepub.com/doi/pdf/10.1177/1071181319631016]

50 Cranford, J. *Incident Response Plan: Frameworks and Steps.* [https://www.crowdstrike.com/cyber security-101/incident-response/incident-response-steps/]

51 Lumu. [https://lumu.io/product/]

52 Stringhini, G, Hulsebos, G, Heyer, T & Vigna, G. "The Psychology of Incident Response: A Literature Review." In Proceedings of the 2017 ACM SIGSAC Conference on Computer and Communications Security, pp. 1511-1524. ACM, 2017

53 Jalali, M et al, *EARS to Cyber Incidents in Health Care* (2019) 26(1) Journal of the American Medical Informatics Association : JAMIA 81

54 Mouratidis, H et al, *Modelling Language for Cyber Security Incident Handling for Critical Infrastructures* (2023) 128 Computers & security 103139

55 Van der Kleij, R et al, *Developing Decision Support for Cyber security Threat and Incident Managers* (2022) 113 Computers & security 102535

56 Ibid

[57] Van der Kleij, et al. *Developing decision support for cyber security threat and incident managers.* Computers & Security, Elsevier Ltd, 2022

[58] Ibid

[59] Ibid

[60] Gardner, H, *Frames of Mind: the Theory of Multiple Intelligences* (Basic Books, 2nd ed., 1993)

[61] DXC. *How response teams can control emotions during high-stress security incidents.* [https://dxc.com/us/en/insights/perspectives/paper/how-response-teams-can-control-emotions-during-high-stress-security-incidents]

[62] ibid

[63] Pappenheim, B. *Managing stress in incident response teams.* [https://www.thecyberfish.com/post/managing-stress-in-incident-response-teams]

[64] Kapko, M. *Incident responders report alarming rates of mental strain.* [https://www.cybersecuritydive.com/news/incident-response-impacts-wellbeing/633593/]

[65] De Witt, J & Meyer, C. *Uncovering Cognitive Biases in Security Decision Making.* [https://www.asisonline.org/security-management-magazine/articles/2022/05/uncovering-cognitive-biases-in-security-decision-making/]

[66] Ibid

[67] NCSC. *Incident Response.* [https://www.ncsc.gov.uk/collection/incident-management/technical-response-capabilities]

[68] Van Der Molen, E., & Van Doesburg, W. L. F. M. (2007). *Human factors in incident response.* In Proceedings of the 2007 International Conference on Availability, Reliability and Security.

[69] Kim, G, Lee, K & Kim, S. *The Psychology of Cyber security Incident Response.* Computers & Security, vol. 83

[70] Humza, N, et al, *Enabling Cybersecurity Incident Response Agility through Dynamic Capabilities: The Role of Real-Time Analytics* [2023] European journal of information systems 1

[71] Pollini, A., Callari, T.C., Tedeschi, A. et al. *Leveraging human factors in cybersecurity: an integrated methodological approach.* Cogn Tech Work 24, 371–390 (2022). https://doi.org/10.1007/s10111-021-00683-y.

[72] Rohan, R, et al. *Understanding of Human Factors in Cybersecurity: A Systematic Literature Review*, 2021 International Conference on Computational Performance Evaluation (ComPE), Shillong, India, 2021, pp. 133-140, doi: 10.1109/ComPE53109.2021.9752358.

73 Encyclopedia Britannica. *Evolutionary psychology | Human Behavior & Adaptation.* , Encyclopedia Britannica, Inc.,
2022, [www.britannica.com/science/evolutionary-psychology]
74 Logpoint. *Behavioral approach to security.*
[https://www.logpoint.com/en/blog/behavioral-approach-to-security/]
75 McLeod, S. *Behaviorism In Psychology.*
[https://www.simplypsychology.org/behaviorism.html]
76 Mutemwa, M & Mtsweni, J. *A Cyber security Architecture That Supports Effective Incident Response* (2022) 21(1) Journal of information warfare 139
77 CAUDIT. *Cybermindz release a new study showing early evidence of burnout in cyber professionals.* (n.d.).
[https://caudit.edu.au/resources/cybermindz-release-a-new-study-showing-early-evidence-of-burnout-in-cyber-professionals/]
78 Posey, C., & Shoss, M. (2022, January 20). *Why Employees Violate Cyber security Policies.* Harvard Business Review.
[https://hbr.org/2022/01/research-why-employees-violate-cyber security-policies]
79 Incyber. *The State of Burnout, a growing concern in the cyber security industry.* (2023, February 27). [https://incyber.org/en/state-burnout-growing-concern-cyber security-industry/]
80 Beyond Blue. *Police and Emergency Services.*
[https://www.beyondblue.org.au/about-us/about-our-work/workplace-mental-health/pes-program]
81 Bada, M & Nurse, J. *The Social and Psychological Impact of Cyber attacks.* [Benson & McAlaney (2019/20) Emerging Cyber Threats and Cognitive Vulnerabilities, Academic Press]
82 Ibid
83 Ibid
84 Sorrentino, A., Peracchio, M. A., & Balducci, C. (2018). *Cyber victimisation and psychological distress: The role of coping strategies.* Journal of Consumer Behaviour, 17(6), 543-551.
85 Attrill-Smith, A., Wesson, C. (2020). *The Psychology of Cybercrime.* In: Holt, T., Bossler, A. (eds) The Palgrave Handbook of International Cybercrime and Cyberdeviance. Palgrave Macmillan, Cham.
86 Al-Ramadhani, M et al. *Ransomware Attacks on Hospitals: Impact and Implications,* in IEEE Security & Privacy, vol. 18, no. 6
87 Phair, N. *Cybercrime in Australia – 20 years of in-action.*
https://www.amazon.com.au/Cybercrime-Australia-20-years-action-ebook/dp/B09MHSGL8Y/ref=sr_1_2?crid=2PF7H553VTWA2&keywords=Ni

gel+Phair&qid=1699313126&s=books&sprefix=nigel+phai%2Cstripbooks%2C314&sr=1-2

[88] Shu, T & Huang, H. *Economic Analysis of Ransomware*. arXiv:1703.06660 [cs.CR], Mar. 2017

[89] ASD. *ASD Cyber Threat Report 2022-2023*. [https://www.cyber.gov.au/about-us/reports-and-statistics/asd-cyber-threat-report-july-2022-june-2023]

[90] CyberReason. *Ransomware: the true cost to business*. [https://www.beobachter.ch/sites/default/files/media/document/cybereason_ransomware_research_2021.pdf]

[91] Halperin, A. *Worried About a Cyberattack? What It Could Cost Your Small Business*. [https://www.businessnewsdaily.com/8475-cost-of-cyberattack.html]

[92] Vasoya, S, Bhavsar, K & Patel, N. (2022). *A systematic literature review on Ransomware attacks*. 10.48550/arXiv.2212.04063.

[93] Emsisoft. *The cost of ransomware in 2020. A country-by-country analysis*. [https://www.emsisoft.com/en/blog/35583/report-the-cost-of-ransomware-in-2020-a-country-by-country-analysis/]

[94] Above N90. CyberReason

[95] IBM. *Cost of a Data Breach Report 2023*. [https://www.ibm.com/reports/data-breach]

[96] Above N90. CyberReason

[97] Above N87. Phair

[98] Above N89. ASD.

[99] Above N88. T. Shu and H. Huang

[100] Chandra NA, Ratna AAP, Ramli K. *Development and Simulation of Cyberdisaster Situation Awareness Models*. Sustainability. 2022; 14(3):1133. [https://doi.org/10.3390/su14031133]

[101] CMA. *Top 3 Benefits of Cyber Incident Response Training*. [https://www.cm-alliance.com/cyber security-blog/top-3-benefits-of-cyber-incident-response-training]

[102] Taylor-Jackson, et al (2020). *Incorporating Psychology into Cyber Security Education: A Pedagogical Approach. In: Bernhard*, M., *et al*. Financial Cryptography and Data Security. FC 2020. Lecture Notes in Computer Science(), vol 12063. Springer, Cham. [https://doi.org/10.1007/978-3-030-54455-3_15]

[103] Bada, M, Sasse, A & Nurse, J. *Cyber Security Awareness Campaigns: Why do they fail to change behaviour?* [https://arxiv.org/abs/1901.02672]

[104] Wiley, A et al. *More than the individual: Examining the relationship between culture and Information Security Awareness.* Computers & Security, Volume 88, January 2020, 101640

[105] Piaget, J. (1971). The theory of stages in cognitive development. In D. R. Green, M. P. Ford, & G. B. Flamer, Measurement and Piaget. McGraw-Hill.

[106] Bandura, A., & Walters, R. H. (1977). Social learning theory. Prentice-Hall.

[107] Bronfenbrenner, U. (2000). *Ecological systems theory.* In A. E. Kazdin (Ed.), Encyclopedia of Psychology (Vol. 3, pp. 129–133). Oxford University Press

[108] Seligman, M. E. P., & Csikszentmihalyi, M. (2000). *Positive psychology: An introduction.* American Psychologist, 55(1), 5–14

[109] Maennel, et al. (2023). *A Multidimensional Cyber Defence Exercise: Emphasis on Emotional, Social, and Cognitive Aspects. SAGE Open, 13*(1).

[110] ISACA. *Incident Response Models.* [https://www.isaca.org/resources/isaca-journal/issues/2020/volume-4/incident-response-models]

[111] Seonghyeon, G & Changhoon L, *Cyber Threat Intelligence Framework for Incident Response in an Energy Cloud Platform* (2021) 10(3) Electronics (Basel) 239

[112] McKinsey. *Follow the leaders: How governments can combat intensifying cyber security risks.* [https://www.mckinsey.com/industries/public-sector/our-insights/follow-the-leaders-how-governments-can-combat-intensifying-cyber security-risks]

[113] Dsousa, S. *Are Cyber Security Incident Response Teams (CSIRTs) Redundant or Can They Be Relevant to International Cyber Security?* (2018) 69(3) Federal communications law journal 201

[114] Ibid

[115] Van der Kleij, R, Kleinhuis, G & Young, H. *Computer Security Incident Response Team Effectiveness: A Needs Assessment* (2017) 8 Frontiers in psychology 2179

[116] Ibid

[117] Ibid

[118] Chen et al. *An Organisational Psychology Perspective to Examining Computer Security Incident Response Teams.* in *IEEE Security & Privacy,* vol. 12, no. 5, pp. 61-67, Sept.-Oct. 2014, doi: 10.1109/MSP.2014.85.

[119] Ibid

[120] Ibid

[121] Valkenburg, B & Bongiovanni, I. *Unravelling the three lines model in cybersecurity: a systematic literature review.*

[https://www.sciencedirect.com/science/article/pii/S0167404824000099]
[122] Kehoe, J. *Cyber security a 'No. 1' risk for company directors: ASIC.* [https://www.afr.com/politics/federal/cyber security-a-number-one-risk-for-company-directors-asic-20230103-p5ca13]
[123] Davies, V. *The psychological impact of phishing attacks on employees.* [https://cybermagazine.com/articles/the-psychological-impact-of-phishing-attacks-on-your-employe]
[124] Marsh Australia. *Cyber insurance market trends 2023.* [www.marsh.com/au/products-services/cyber-insurance/insights/cyber-insurance-market-trends-2023.html]
[125] Parrant, M. *Company Directors Risk More Than Their Customer's Data From Cyber Attacks.* [https://aoninsights.com.au/company-directors-risk-more-than-their-customers-data-from-cyber attacks/]

www.ingramcontent.com/pod-product-compliance
Lightning Source LLC
Chambersburg PA
CBHW070113260726
48658CB00001B/107